Progress Relational Data Modeling and Schema Design

Biju George

Sandy Davis

Steve Hoberman

Align > Refine > Design Series

Technics Publications

Published by:

115 Linda Vista, Sedona, AZ 86336 USA
https://www.TechnicsPub.com

Edited by Sadie Hoberman
Cover design by Lorena Molinari

First Printing 2024
Copyright © 2024 by Technics Publications

ISBN, print ed.   9781634622707
ISBN, Kindle ed.   9781634622714
ISBN, PDF ed.   9781634622738

Library of Congress Control Number: 2024937114

Contents

About the Book

My daughter can make a mean brownie. She starts with a store-bought brownie mix and adds chocolate chips, apple cider vinegar, and other "secret" ingredients to make her own unique delicious brownie.

Building a robust database design meeting the needs of users requires a similar approach. The store-bought brownie mix represents a proven recipe for success. Likewise, there are data modeling practices that have proven successful over many decades. The chocolate chips and other secret ingredients represent the special additions that lead to an exceptional product. Progress® MarkLogic has a number of special design considerations, much like the chocolate chips. Combining proven data modeling practices with Progress® MarkLogic design-specific practices creates a series of data models representing powerful communication tools, greatly improving the opportunities for an exceptional design and application.

In fact, each book in the Align > Refine > Design series covers conceptual, logical, and physical data modeling for a specific database product, combining the best of data modeling practices with solution-specific design considerations. It is a winning combination.

My daughter's first few brownies were not a success, although as the proud (and hungry) dad, I ate them anyway—and they were still pretty tasty. It took practice to get the brownie to come out amazing. We need practice on the modeling side as well. Therefore, each book in the series follows the same animal shelter case study, allowing you to see the modeling techniques applied to reinforce your learning.

If you want to learn how to build multiple database solutions, read all the books in the series. Once you read one, you can pick up the techniques for another database solution even quicker.

Some say my first word was "data." I have been a data modeler for over 30 years and have taught variations of my **Data Modeling Master Class** since 1992—currently up to the 10th Edition! I have written nine books on data modeling, including *The Rosedata Stone* and *Data Modeling Made Simple.* I review data models using my Data Model Scorecard® technique. I am the founder of the Design Challenges group, creator of the Data Modeling Institute's Data Modeling Certification exam, Conference Chair of the Data Modeling Zone conferences, director of Technics Publications, lecturer at Columbia University, and recipient of the Data Administration Management Association (DAMA) International Professional Achievement Award.

Thinking of my daughter's brownie analogy, I have perfected the store-bought brownie recipe. That is, I know how to model. However, I am not an expert in every database solution.

That is why each book in this series combines my proven data modeling practices with database solution experts. So, for this book, Biju George, Sandy Davis, and I are making the brownie together. I work on the store-bought brownie piece, and Sandy and Biju work on adding the chocolate chips and other delicious ingredients. Sandy and Biju are MarkLogic thought leaders.

Biju George is a seasoned professional with over 25 years of progressive experience catering to the critical technology needs of enterprise customers across various industries such as insurance, healthcare, finance, and logistics. As a Sales and Solutions Engineer, Biju specializes in working with large enterprises, leveraging his expertise to resolve complex data problems using MarkLogic, the leading enterprise-hardened schema-agnostic database platform in the global market. Biju has been working with Progress® MarkLogic since 2018.

Sandy Davis is an Enterprise Data Architect at a major Class 1 railroad in the United States. Sandy has been working with Relational (SQL) and NoSQL databases in the roles of developer, database administrator, and data architect since 1989. Sandy has been leading the deployment and adoption of MarkLogic since 2018.

Several of the topics covered in this book, such as Embedding versus Referencing, along with many of the Patterns, are common across document-style databases. Some of the content in these sections is inspired by principles outlined by Daniel Coupal in his renowned work, *MongoDB Data Modeling and Schema Design*. This book demonstrates how these principles align with prevalent document database modeling methodologies and showcases their applicability to Progress® MarkLogic.

We hope our tag team approach shows you how to model any Progress® MarkLogic solution. Particularly for those with experience in data modeling of relational databases, the book provides a bridge from the traditional methods to the very different way we model to leverage the benefits of NoSQL in general and Progress® Progress(R) MarkLogic in particular.

Note that any reference to MarkLogic in this book pertains to Progress® MarkLogic[1].

We authored this book for two audiences:

- Data architects and modelers who need to expand their modeling skills to include MarkLogic. That is, those of us who know how to make a store-bought brownie but are looking for those secret additions like chocolate chips.

- Database administrators and developers who know MarkLogic but need to expand their modeling skills. That is, those of us who know the value of chocolate chips and other ingredients but need to learn how to combine these ingredients with those store-bought brownie mixes.

This book contains a foundational introduction followed by three approach-driven chapters. Think of the introduction as making that store-built brownie and the subsequent chapters as adding chocolate chips and other yummy ingredients. More on these four sections:

- **Chapter 1: Data Models in a DBMS (database management system).** This chapter will explain how database management systems support different model types, including relational, key-value, wide column, graph, and document.

- **Chapter 2: The JSON Document Model.** This chapter will provide an overview of JSON, along

---

[1] https://www.progress.com/marklogic

with its benefits and an explanation of related concepts, including polymorphism.

- **Chapter 3: About MarkLogic**. This chapter will describe the unique approaches MarkLogic takes for managing enterprise data. Learn how MarkLogic supports storing data in different formats and how to present data in one format in another.

- **Chapter 4: About Data Models**. This overview covers the three modeling characteristics of precise, minimal, and visual; the three model components of entities, relationships, and attributes; the three model levels of conceptual (align), logical (refine), and physical (design); and the three modeling perspectives of relational, dimensional, and query. By the end of this modeling overview, you will know data modeling concepts and how to approach any data modeling assignment. This chapter will be useful to database administrators and developers who need a foundation in data modeling, as well as data architects and data modelers who need a modeling refresher.

- **Chapter 5: Align**. This chapter will explain the data modeling align phase. We explain the purpose of aligning our business vocabulary, introduce our animal shelter case study, and then walk through the align approach. This chapter will be useful for both audiences, architects/modelers, and database administrators/developers.

- **Chapter 6: Refine**. This chapter will explain the data modeling refine phase. We explain the purpose of refine, refine the model for our animal shelter case study, and then walk through the refine approach. This chapter will be useful for both audiences, architects/modelers, and database administrators/developers.

- **Chapter 7: Design**. This chapter will explain the data modeling design phase. We explain the purpose of design, design the model for our animal shelter case study, and then walk through the design approach. This chapter will be useful for both audiences, architects/modelers, and database administrators/developers.

We end each chapter with three tips and three takeaways. We aim to write as concisely yet comprehensively as possible to make the most of your time.

Most data models throughout the book were created using Hackolade Studio (https://hackolade.com) and are accessible for reference at https://github.com/hackolade/books along with additional sample data models to play with.

Let's begin!

Biju, Sandy, and Steve

CHAPTER 1

About Database Models

We can categorize databases in different ways, such as by the database model supported. The database model is the logical structure of the data items and their relationships. Many databases support only a single database model. As the name suggests, a multi-model database supports multiple models on a single integrated backend. Multi-model databases store, query, and index data from different models. This chapter will explain the five basic types of database models: relational, key-value, wide column, graph, and document.

Relational

Of all the data models, the relational model is the most well-known. The relational model is an intellectual concept created by Edgar F. Codd in the 1980s as a general model of data. The basic concepts include relations, attributes, tuples, keys, and foreign keys.

From a logical perspective, data is stored in a collection of distinctly named entities where each entity has a specified set of uniquely named attributes. Entities are tabular structures that represent real-world objects or concepts, like customers, products, or orders, and are essentially the building blocks of the database. The rows in an entity represent instances of that entity, with each row identified by a unique primary key that consists of one or more attributes. A relational database is a materialization of the relational model. The physical implementation of entities and attributes in a relational database turn into tables and columns.

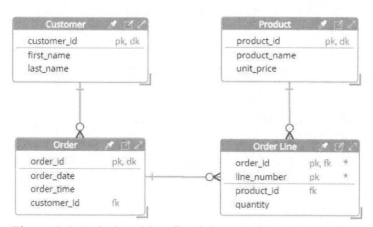

Figure 1.1: Relational has fixed dense tables with flexible queries and joins.

Normalization produces parent-child relationships across entities implemented through foreign keys. A foreign key is where the key columns from one entity (the parent) are stored in another entity (the child). The database management system enforces foreign key relationships, which also enforces data integrity. Foreign keys are what put the *relational* in the relational database.

A variation of the relational model is the dimensional model. The dimensional model is the most popular modeling technique in data warehousing because of its simplicity. The dimensional model identifies three types of tables:

- Fact tables that record the measures of business events (such as sales) or states.
- Dimension tables that represent the who, what, where, and when of business events.
- Bridge tables that resolve many-to-many relationships between a fact and a dimension.

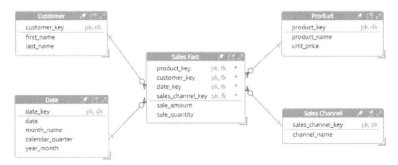

Figure 1.2: Dimensional (Kimball Data Warehousing).

If you are not familiar with the notation used in the preceding diagrams, this will be discussed in detail in the *About Data Models* chapter.

Key-value

The key-value model is the simplest of all the NoSQL data models. The data *value* being stored is assigned a unique key. A hashing mechanism is used such that given a key, the database can quickly retrieve the associated value. The keys can be any type of object but are typically a string. The values are generally blobs (i.e., a sequence of bytes that the database does not interpret). Key-value databases have no query language because data retrieval is a simple matter of using get, put, and delete commands.

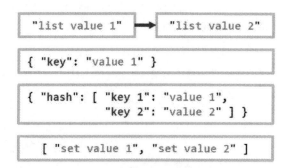

Figure 1.3: Key-Value with pre-defined data structures, no queries.

Applications that use key-value databases must frequently know and understand the data content in the value field, thus the data structure is often pre-defined. It may still be desirable to document the content of key-value stores with a data model if the value is a complex object (e.g., a JSON document representing the content of a shopping cart.)

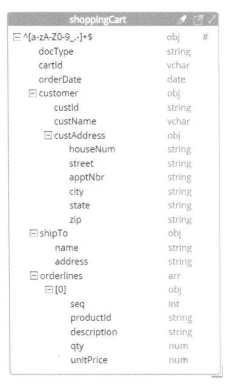

Figure 1.4: Model of key-value pre-defined data structures.

The simplicity of the key-value model makes these types of databases capable of storing massive amounts of data while providing fast response times even when handling exceptionally large workloads. Key-value databases are highly partitionable and allow for extreme horizontal scaling. The main use cases for key-value databases are user preferences, user profiles, and shopping carts.

Wide column

A wide-column database (also known as a column-family database) stores data in a column-family format. A column family is a collection of rows and columns, where each row has a unique key and each column has a name, value, and timestamp. With wide-column databases, columns are always optional (not mandatory or null) and a row column with no data does not exist in storage. This is in contrast to relational databases where each table row has the same number of columns and columns that are null (no value) are represented with a null value indicator.

Key	chanel_type	cust_id	order_id	timestamp	cust_name	product_id	qty	price	amount
1	WebPortal	1013	W75301	20230417	Sandy Davis	19801-21	4	2.75	11.00
2	WebPortal	1013	W75301	20230417	Sandy Davis	79102-57	2	21.25	42.50
3	Retail Store	3761	R218976	20130521	Biju George	48910-76	6	7.99	47.94
4	Retail Store	4732	R375383	20230528	Steve Hoberman	79102-57	2	21.25	42.50

Figure 1.5: Wide Column, with dense tables with fixed queries, no joins.

The wide-column is similar to the key-value in that each row has a key composed of one or more columns. Some wide-column databases support a SQL-like query language, but SQL joins are not supported. Wide-column databases typically excel at ingesting data at a very high rate.

A wide column table can be specified in a data model but depending the particular technology platform, enforcement of data types and other column constraints varies.

Graph

Ironically, the graph data model focuses on relationships. Like the relational model, the graph model has strong ties to mathematics. A graph in mathematics is a representation of a network consisting of vertices (also called nodes) and the edges that connect them (also called links). Visually, a graph model appears as ovals or circles with lines connecting them.

In a graph-based data model, a node can represent a data entity, data element, or any other type of object to be tracked. The relationship or association between nodes is represented by one or more edges. The edges are stored directly, as these are the first-class elements of the data model.

The edges in a graph model can be directed or undirected. In a directed graph, the edges have a specific direction, which means there is a distinction between each edge's start and end points. In contrast, undirected graphs do not have a specific direction for their edges, meaning that each edge is bidirectional and can be traversed in either direction.

There are two popular types of graph models: RDF graph and labeled property graph.

RDF graph

The RDF (Resource Description Framework) is a W3C standard framework for describing resources on the Web, also known as the Semantic Web. According to Tim

Berners-Lee, "The Semantic Web is an extension of the current web in which information is given well-defined meaning, better-enabling computers and people to work in cooperation."[2] The primary representation for data/information is called a *resource* by the W3C and in REST APIs (Application Programming Interface).[3,4] A resource can be almost anything, such as physical things, documents, abstract concepts, numbers, and strings. The term resource is synonymous with *concept* or *entity* as described later in the *About Data Models* chapter. The RDF data model is based on the idea of making statements about resources using expressions in the form of *subject-predicate-object*, known as triples.

- **Subject** is a resource being described by the triple.
- **Predicate** describes the relationship between the subject and the object.
- **Object** is a resource that is related to the subject.

Since RDF is a web language, it uses URIs (Uniform Resource Identifiers) to identify each component of the triple. The following are some abstract examples of triples.

- URI-1 (Tony) URI-2 (buys) URI-3 (coffee maker)

---

[2] https://www.w3.org/RDF/Metalog/docs/sw-easy.

[3] W3C,
https://www.w3.org/DesignIssues/Generic.html#:~:text=A%20%22resource%22%20is%20a%20conceptual,version%20of%20an%20Internet%20RFC.

[4] Representational State Transfer (REST), Chapter 5, https://ics.uci.edu/~fielding/pubs/dissertation/rest_arch_style.htm#sec_5_2_1_1.

- URI-1 (Tony) URI-4 (buys on) URI-5 (Amazon)
- URI-6 (ACME) URI-7 supplies (URI-3) coffee maker

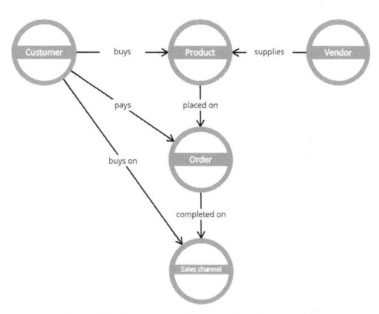

Figure 1.6: RDF Graph can have unlimited relationships.

The name RDF Graph comes from the fact that triples can be linked. That is, the object of one triple being the subject of another triple, forming a graph-like representation with nodes and edges (the lines linking nodes). Also, since RDF is about semantics or the meaning of information (the semantic web), a *Semantic Data Model* is a data model that is comprised of RDF triples. With MarkLogic being a multi-model database that supports RDF, we will discuss the *Semantic Graph Pattern* later in the book.

One of the more well know RDF implementations is DBpedia[5], a crowd-sourced community effort to extract structured information from Wikipedia and make this information available on the Web. At the time of this writing, the DBpedia triple store consists of several billion RDF triples covering domains such as geographic information, people, companies, online communities, films, music, books, and scientific publications.

RDF-star[6] is an extension to RDF that provides a way for one triple to refer to another triple by treating it as a single entity. As an extension, RDF-star supplements RDF but doesn't replace it. RDF-star allows for *nesting* or *embedding* triples, and thus an entire triple can become the subject of a second triple. This enables the creation of relationships not just between two entities in a graph, but between triples and entities, or triples and triples. The embedding of triples also allows properties to be added to edges in a graph such as scores, weights, metadata, and temporal aspects. Overall, RDF-star reduces the maintenance burden for RDF graphs.

Property graph

A property graph, also called a labeled property graph, allows properties (attributes) to be stored on both nodes and edges.

---

[5] https://www.dbpedia.org/about/.

[6] https://www.w3.org/2021/12/rdf-star.html

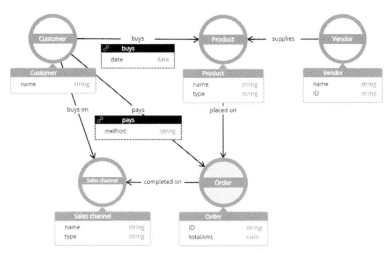

Figure 1.7: Property Graph contains nodes and edges with properties.

Attributes can be any property that gives details of a data entity or a relationship. Property graphs get their name from their capability to include properties associated with nodes and edges denoted as key-value pairs.

Document

The document model stores data in the form of JSON and XML documents. JSON and XML documents contain a list of properties (attribute-value pairs) that describe and provide context to the document. A document is the basic unit of data (like a row in a relational database) and can include nesting to represent complex data structures. Documents do not have a predetermined structure. Instead, they have an internal, self-defined structure. The structure of a document can be described by schema languages such as JSON Schema[i] and XML Schema Definition (XSD).[ii]

A note about terminology

In data modeling, an attribute identifies, names, or defines a characteristic or property of an entity type. Some refer to JSON as a key-value structure, but a *key* implies uniqueness and keys may be repeated in JSON documents, thus the preference for using *attribute-value* in this book. An attribute is often generically called a *data element* and are interchangeable terms in this book.

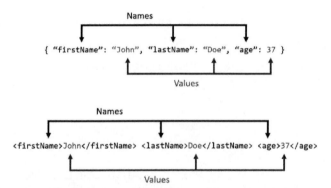

Figure 1.8: JSON and XML attribute-value pairs.

How JSON and XML are similar

- Both JSON and XML are *self-describing* and, therefore, human-readable
- Both JSON and XML are hierarchical
- Both JSON and XML can be parsed and used by lots of programming languages

- Both JSON and XML can be fetched with an http request

How JSON is different than XML

- JSON doesn't use end tags
- JSON has limited data types
- JSON is quicker to read and write
- JSON can use arrays
- JavaScript dot notation used to navigate document

How XML is different than JSON

- XML has namespaces to allow for common data structures and re-use
- XML supports URIs
- XML has rigorous data types
- XPath and XQuery are W3C standard languages for navigating and searching documents

```
{
    "custId": 1013,
    "customer": {
        "lastName": "Doe",
        "firstName": "John"
        },
    "items": [
      { "productId": "19821-01",
        "qty": 4,
        "unitPrice": 2.75,
        "amount": 11.00
      },
      { "productId": "79102-03",
        "qty": 2,
        "unitPrice": 21.25,
        "amount": 42.50
      }
    ]
}
```

Figure 1.9: Sample JSON order document.

```
<order>
  <custId>1013</custId>
  <customer>
      <lastName>Doe</lastName>
      <firstName>John</firstName>
  </customer>
  <items>
    <item>
        <productId>19821-01</productId>
        <qty>4</qty>
        <unitPrice>2.75</unitPrice>
        <amount>11.00</amount>
    </item>
    <item>
        <productId>79102-03</productId>
        <qty>2</qty>
        <unitPrice>21.25</unitPrice>
        <amount>42.50</amount>
    </item>
  </items>
</order>
```

Figure 1.10: Sample XML Order document (Note bloat vs JSON due to end tags).

The two most significant differences are:

1. XML has to be parsed with an XML parser, while JSON can be parsed by a standard JavaScript function

2. JSON syntax is far less bloated than XML

Sample order doc	
custId	num
⊟ customer	obj
lastName	string
firstName	string
⊟ items	arr
⊟ [0]	obj
productId	string
qty	num
unitPrice	num
amount	num

Figure 1.11: Data model for sample order document.

Data types

JSON provides a few basic data types.

- string
- number
- integer
- object
- array
- Boolean
- null

XML provides a very robust set of data types.

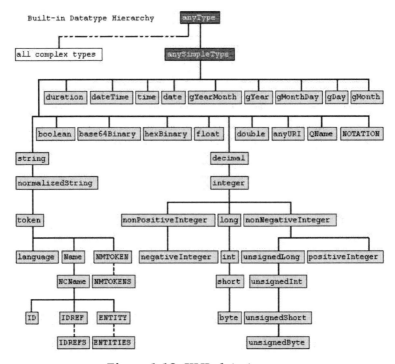

Figure 1.12: XML data types.

Summary

This chapter provided a high-level understanding of the different database model types. There is no single model that works well for every use case. By necessity, organizations will require more than one model to support diverse types of data and workloads. Polyglot persistence is the idea of using multiple models in combination in an application.

The design of any database application requires the design of data structure(s) that make the application performant and meet business requirements. To this end, data modeling tools can be extremely useful in facilitating data design through visualization, which in turn promotes communication and understanding among all involved in the development process.

Many data model types we have discussed use standard diagraming notations for visually expressing a model. For example, the relational model has several notations supported by data modeling tools, with Barker and Information Engineering (IE) being two of the more popular. While not visualization notations, XSD and JSON Schema[7] are languages used to express the organizational structure of XML and JSON documents through which data modeling tools can produce visual data models. One such tool, Hackolade Studio[8], was used to create most of the data model visuals (diagrams)

---

[7] https://json-schema.org/.

[8] https://hackolade.com.

in this book. Hackolade pioneered Polyglot Data Modeling, which is data modeling for polyglot data persistence and data exchanges. With Hackolade's Metadata-as-Code strategy, data models are co-located with application code in Git repositories as they evolve and are published to business-facing data catalogs to ensure a shared understanding of the meaning and context of your data.

The primary focus of this book is the design and modeling of documents. Considering that JSON has evolved to be the standard format for storing data in documents, it is the format on which we will focus going forward.

About MarkLogic

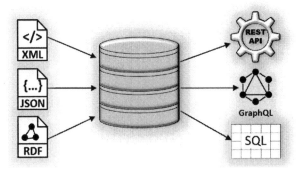

T his chapter describes the unique approaches MarkLogic takes for managing enterprise data. We discuss how MarkLogic supports storing data in different formats and how data in one format can presented in another.

MarkLogic originated in 2001 as an XML database to enable organizations to integrate, store, manage, and search their data, similar to Google Search.

MarkLogic is one of the earliest entries in the NoSQL database realm. According to Keith Foote[9] in an article on DATAVERSITY, "the acronym NoSQL was first used in 1998 by Carlo Strozzi while naming his lightweight, open-source *relational* database that did not use SQL.

---

[9] Keith Foote, A Brief History of Non-Relational Databases, 2018, DATAVERSITY, https://www.dataversity.net/a-brief-history-of-non-relational-databases/.

The name came up again in 2009 when Eric Evans and Johan Oskarsson used it to describe non-relational databases."

NoSQL also refers to databases that store data in a means other than the tabular relations used in relational databases. NoSQL databases often do not require the structure of the data (schema) to be defined up-front and provide the ability to store and manage large sets of unstructured or semi-structured data. Over the years, the term NoSQL has evolved from *No SQL* or *Non-SQL* to *Not Only SQL* to reflect that many non-relational databases now support SQL-like query languages.

Today, MarkLogic is a multi-model database along with an embedded search engine and application services layer, all in one product. Thus, you don't need to 'bolt on' vendor add-ons or third-party products with all the integration code and separate update schedules that implies.

Multi-model features of MarkLogic

We should not mistake the multi-model capabilities of MarkLogic for polyglot persistence. An application melds various data models in polyglot persistence, often relying on distinct technologies to support these disparate models. To illustrate, JSON documents find their home in one document store, XML documents reside in a separate XML store, binaries stored in an object store, and network data within a graph store. This approach results in the creation of data silos, adding significant complexity to the technology stack's data layer.

In contrast, a multi-model database is one that supports multiple data models in their natural form within a single, integrated backend and uses data standards and query standards appropriate to each model. Queries are extended or combined to provide seamless access across all the supported data models. The core database product includes indexing, parsing, and processing standards appropriate to the data model.

MarkLogic offers native storage for JSON, XML, text, RDF triples, geospatial data, and binaries (such as PDFs, images, and videos) while providing a cohesive search and query interface. This simplifies data architecture significantly.

MarkLogic goes beyond multi-model by seamlessly integrating a robust search engine and application server. This synergy ensures that all documents in JSON, XML, and text formats are automatically indexed, rendering them instantly available for comprehensive full-text searches. This innovative approach obviates the necessity of including a separate indexing and search engine within the data layer. Furthermore, the server's application services component readily exposes REST-like APIs out-of-the-box, providing the flexibility to develop new REST services effortlessly. The cumulative effect of these features streamlines the process from data ingestion to making it readily searchable, accomplishing this task in a matter of minutes, if not seconds.

Does data modeling matter in MarkLogic?

MarkLogic's schema-agnostic framework and versatile multi-model capabilities facilitate the seamless integration of diverse data in various formats. However, a crucial aspect, particularly pertinent to the content of this technical book, must be carefully considered. While data modeling is not required up front for data ingestion into MarkLogic, experience has shown that not understanding the data context and semantics (meaning of the data) impacts processing and consumption, which has been a recipe for failure. Therefore, the key to effective data modeling in MarkLogic is to understand that data modeling should be incremental and geared towards the needs of your deliverables. This applies to the development of all application types, such as operational, analytic, and data integration. Tips using this approach include:

- For analytic and data integration use cases, it is not required that every document property/attribute be modeled. This promotes strategic and targeted data modeling.

- Data can be modeled after it is loaded, as well as before. Hackolade Studio can be very useful for quickly generating an initial data model from data that has been loaded into MarkLogic.

- Evaluate the kind of data access your consumers need. The data elements that need to be explicitly modeled include those involved in search operations, those that need to be aggregated, and anything that needs to be harmonized (different field names for the same thing, different units, etc.). This significance stems from the fact that consumption, typically through an API or as a search result, requires a clear understanding of the response structure for effective use.

In contrast, if the objective of consumption is merely to retrieve documents in their original stored form, modeling becomes less critical. Query patterns should influence the modeling approach when structuring documents. MarkLogic, rooted in search-engine-style indexing techniques, treats a database query akin to a search operation. Consequently, the storage structure of documents should optimize efficiency for search operations. This book's subsequent sections delve into the MarkLogic storage model, illuminating the essential considerations for effective data modeling.

Storage model

Under the covers, MarkLogic stores documents as compressed trees, based on the well-known XPath Data Model. This model is sufficiently featured to represent all sorts of documents, including plain-text and JSON. For example, take the XML document in Figure 2.1.

```
<doc><title>My doc</title><body>Some text.</body></doc>
```
Figure 2.1: Sample XML document.

It is represented in MarkLogic as a tree structure, shown in Figure 2.2.

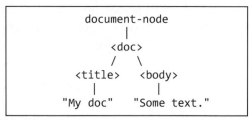

Figure 2.2: XML document as a tree structure in MarkLogic.

The advantage of storing documents in XML format is that you can query the tree structure using XPath expressions such as /doc/title. With MarkLogic, you can perform searches that are aware of and can be qualified by this tree structure.

So, how is a text document like this one represented?

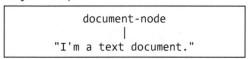

Figure 2.3: Sample text document.

Well, since every document is a tree, this one is too (albeit a simple one).

```
            document-node
                 |
        "I'm a text document."
```

Figure 2.4: Text document as a tree structure in MarkLogic.

Binary documents are also (trivial) trees, like text documents. But in this case, MarkLogic extends the XPath model to include binary nodes. These are special and can only occur as singular children of the document node. For example, the storage of a JPG file would look like this:

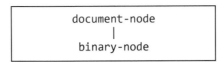

Figure 2.5: JPG file as a tree structure in MarkLogic.

MarkLogic stores binary data as is (without additional compression) and provides a mechanism for storing the binary data externally, outside of the database as well.

For a JSON document, the nodes below the document node represent JSON objects, arrays, text, number, Boolean, and null values. Only JSON documents contain object, array, number, Boolean, and null node types. For example, Figure 2.6 shows a JSON object and its tree representation when stored in the database as a JSON document. If the object were an in-memory construct rather than a document, the root document node would not be present.

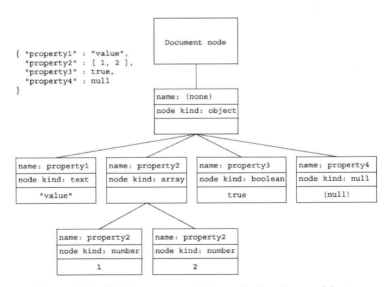

Figure 2.6: JSON representation of a business object.

Document URI

Recall the origin of MarkLogic as an XML database. XML supports namespaces, an abstract domain to which a collection of element and attribute names can be assigned. The purpose of a namespace is to ensure that all the objects in the domain have unique names so that they can be easily identified. In XML, a namespace is identified or named by a Uniform Resource Identifier (URI). URIs are used widely to identify resources used by web technologies. URIs may be used to identify anything, including real-world objects, such as people and places, concepts, or information resources, such as web pages and books.

MarkLogic uses a URI as a document's key, which you choose when you insert a document into the database. Each document has a unique URI within the database. You use this URI to retrieve or refer to the document. Beyond the document URI, MarkLogic maintains some additional metadata associated with each document, including properties, permissions, and quality.

Document organization

How does MarkLogic organize documents in the database? Logically, MarkLogic provides two concepts: Collections and Directories. You can think of collections as unordered sets. If you have a notion of tag as well, that may help. Collections may hold multiple documents and documents can belong to multiple collections.

Directories are similar in concept to the notion of directories or folders in file systems. They are hierarchical and membership is implicit based on the path syntax of URIs.

Directories

Directories in MarkLogic are simply conventions reflected by document URIs. There is no resource corresponding to a directory that exists in the database. Internally, a directory is stored as a properties document. Like a document, a directory has a URI, but the URI must end in a forward slash (/). Directories seem a more natural way to organize documents because they are analogous to filesystem directories.

Directories can have properties such as permissions and last modified timestamps. You can also put your own properties on the directory, which can be quite handy for assigning properties that are common to a group of documents.

You can control the documents users see by controlling access at the directory level and assign a default permission level on a directory that all its children documents will inherit.

Collections

Collections are described as part of the W3C XQuery specification, but their implementation is undefined. MarkLogic has chosen to emphasize collections as a powerful and high-performance mechanism for selecting sets of documents against which queries can be processed.

A collection in MarkLogic is simply a group of documents. A collection can contain an extremely large set of documents, and it is possible to assign documents with different schema definitions to the same collection. A document can be a member of multiple collections, which helps organize the documents for better access. From a relational perspective, you can think of documents and collections having a many-to-many relationship as shown in Figure 2.7. If you are not familiar with diagram notation, this will be discussed in detail in the *About Data Models* chapter. In a nutshell, the *crow's feet* at the ends of the relationship line indicates *many*, while the circle indicates *optional*, and the bar means *required*. The relationship can be stated as follows:

- Each Document may have one or more Collection(s)
- Each Collection must have one or more Document(s)

Figure 2.7: Conceptual relationship of Document to Collection in MarkLogic.

Collections are implemented as if there is a hidden JSON *collection* property or XML *<collection>* element in each document for every collection to which the document belongs. So, if a document belongs to ten collections, it is as if there are ten hidden *collection/ <collection>* elements in the document with the names of the ten collections to which it belongs.

The fundamental database cost for collection metadata is the number of collections each document belongs to, times the number of documents, along with the index for fast lookup. Fundamentally, having one collection with a million documents is about the same as having a million collections, each with one document.

For example, assume there is a document for Auto Policy and another for Home Policy. Both documents can be in a *Policy* collection. Additionally, the Auto Policy can be in *Auto* collection and the Home Policy can be in *Home* collection. When searching all policies during query time, we can use the *Policy* collection as part of the query filter. We can use the *Auto* collection to scope the query for searches involving only auto policies.

Having a large number of collections is a great way of organizing documents. The collection mechanism in MarkLogic is very scalable. You can easily have as many collections as documents, and their use is encouraged.

The key differences in using collections to organize documents versus using directories are:

- Collections do not require member documents to conform to any URI patterns. They are not hierarchical, whereas directories are hierarchical. Any document can belong to any collection, and any document can also belong to multiple collections.

- You can delete all documents in a collection with the xdmp:collection-delete function. Similarly, you can delete all documents in a directory (as well as all recursive subdirectories and any documents in those directories) with the xdmp:directory-delete function.

- You cannot set properties on a collection yet you can on a directory.

- Except for the fact that you can use both collections and directories to organize documents, collections are unrelated to directories.

CHAPTER 3

The JSON Document Model

{ JSON }

This chapter provides an overview of JSON, along with its benefits and an explanation of related concepts, including polymorphism.

A JSON document typically represents a business entity or business event such as customer, order, product, vendor, order shipped, etc. As such, JSON provides two constructs to organize data to mimic the physical aspects of a business document.

A JSON document consists of at least one object that contains zero, one, or more name-value pairs, also called properties. Curly braces { } surround the object and every property is separated by a comma. The order of the properties is irrelevant.

A JSON array allows for a list of items. An array is an ordered list of items enclosed in square brackets [ ]. The items can be any valid JSON data type, including another array, an object, a string, a number, a Boolean, or a null. Each item in the array is separated by a comma.

```
["apple", "banana", "orange", "grape"]
```

Figure 3.1: Array of strings.

Within a JSON document, you can combine objects and arrays at will, as shown in Figure 3.2.

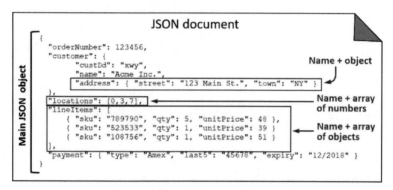

Figure 3.2: JSON document composition.

For example, you may use an array of objects to embed another table into a collection. The array models the one-to-many or many-to-many relationship between the two tables. Typically, the name is static in a JSON name-value pair. It is also possible to have variable names for the property, as shown in Figure 3.3.

```
{
    "followers": {
        "abc123": {
            "name": "John Doe",
            "sports": ["tennis"]
        },
        "xyz987": {
            "name": "Joe Blow",
            "sports": ["cycling", "football"]
        }
    }
}
```

Figure 3.3: Variable names for properties.

This advanced feature, sometimes called *pattern properties* or *unpredictable keys*, is a special case of the attribute pattern described later in the book. Hackolade Studio correctly maintains and also detects these structures during the schema inference of a reverse-engineering process, but these unusual structures challenge traditional SQL and BI tools.

Grouping data in JSON with hierarchical subobjects and arrays provides several benefits:

- **Improved data organization**: nesting related data with subobjects and arrays makes it easier to understand, navigate, query, and manipulate data.

- **Flexibility**: a more flexible data model can evolve and adapt to changing requirements more easily.

- **Improved performance**: embedding subobjects within a parent document can improve performance by reducing the number of I/O requests (reducing the number of documents to return) to retrieve the same data.

- **Data integrity**: by keeping related data together, for example, each order can contain an array of cart items. This way, it is clear that the orders and items are related, and it is also easy to update all related data when required, as well as perform cascading deletes.

- **Developer convenience**: by aggregating structures to match objects for manipulation in object-oriented programming, developers are more efficient by avoiding what's known as *object impedance mismatch* which is a common issue when working with relational databases.

Let us use the simple example of an order to fully visualize the above benefits and why users embrace the document model as an intuitive alternative to traditional relational database structures.

With a relational database respecting the rules of normalization, we split the different components of an order into different tables at storage time. When retrieving the data, joins allow us to reassemble the different pieces for processing, display, or reporting. This is counter-intuitive for the common human (i.e., someone not trained in Third Normal Form) and expensive in terms of performance, particularly at scale. See Figure 3.4.

However, with a JSON document, all the pieces of information that belong together are stored and retrieved in a single document, an example appearing in Figure 3.5.

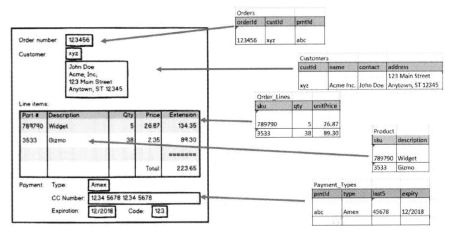

Figure 3.4: Relation representation of a business object.

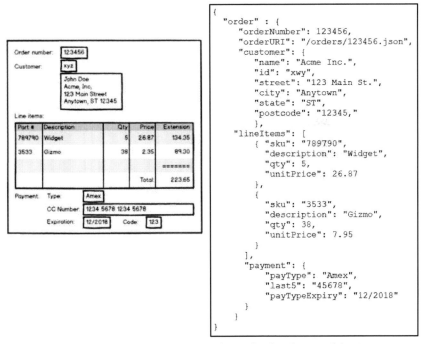

Figure 3.5: JSON representation of a business object.

Nesting can provide the benefits described above, but it can also sometimes make data more complex and harder to work with if it's not properly organized and structured. And since there are no rules of normalization to serve as guardrails, data modeling is even more important than with relational databases.

Nesting subobjects and arrays to denormalize data to represent relationships can also increase the storage requirements. Still, with minimal storage costs these days, this drawback is often considered marginal.

Hackolade Studio uses JSON Schema as an internal notation mechanism, so it dynamically generates JSON Schema for structures created with the tool without the user needing to be familiar with the JSON Schema syntax.

Figure 3.6: Model of a JSON business object.

To decide whether to use or avoid, developers should weigh the benefits and drawbacks of nesting data and make an informed decision. Later in the Design chapter, we will discuss different schema design patterns to help make informed decisions.

Polymorphism

Polymorphism in JSON refers to the ability of a JSON object to take on multiple forms.

Fields with multiple data types

The simplest case of polymorphism in JSON is when a field can have different data types, for example:

```
{
  "raceResults": [
      {
        "Position": 1,
        "Driver": "Lewis Hamilton"
      },
      {
        "Position": 2,
        "Driver": "Max Verstappen"
      },
      {
        "Position": "DNF",
        "Driver": "Charles Leclerc"
      }
  ]
}
```

The "Position" field can have different data types (numeric for rank or string for non-rank status such as *DNS* (Did Not Start), *DNF* (Did Not Finish), or *DSQ* (Disqualified)) depending on the race result.

Multiple document types in a JSON collection

Recall from the *About MarkLogic* chapter that JSON documents may be grouped together into a collection. JSON documents in a collection may share a common subject or have a similar schema. A more complex case of polymorphism is when different documents in the same schema collection have different shapes, similar to table inheritance in relational databases. Specifically, it refers to the ability of a JSON object to have different properties or fields, depending on the type of data it represents.

For example, consider a collection for bank accounts. Several types of bank accounts are possible: checking, savings, and loan. There is a structure common to all types and a structure specific to each type. For example, a document for a checking account might look like this:

```
{
  "accountNumber": "123456789",
  "balance": 1000,
  "accountType": "checking",
  "accountDetails": {
    "minimumBalance": 100,
    "overdraftLimit": 500
  }
}
```

Another document for a savings account might look like this:

```
{
 "accountNumber": "987654321",
 "balance": 5000,
 "accountType": "savings",
 "accountDetails": {
   "interestRate": 0.05,
   "interestEarned": 115.26
 }
}
```

And for a loan account, a document might look like this:

```
{
 "accountNumber": "567890123",
 "balance": -5916.06,
 "accountType": "loan",
 "accountDetails": {
   "loanAmount": 10000,
   "term": 36,
   "interestRate": 1.5,
   "monthlyPmt": 291.71
 }
}
```

This flexible and dynamic structure is very convenient and eliminates the need for separate tables or wide tables that would quickly become unmanageable at scale.

However, this flexibility can also create challenges when querying or manipulating the data, as it requires applications to account for data types and structure variations. Without going into details at this stage, Figure 3.7 shows a single schema for these documents.

Account		
accountNumber	pk	string
dateOpened		date
balance		dbl
accountType		string
⊟ anyOf		ch
⊟ [0] checking		sub
minimumBalance		dec
overdraftLimit		int
⊟ [1] savings		sub
interestRate		dec
interestEarned		dbl
⊟ [2] loan		sub
loanAmount		dbl
term		int
interestRate		dec
monthlyPmt		dbl

Figure 3.7: Single schema.

For those familiar with traditional data modeling, the above would be represented with subtypes and could result in table inheritance, as shown in Figure 3.8.

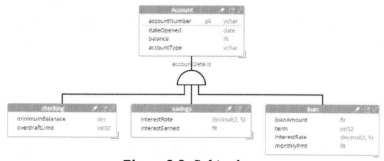

Figure 3.8: Subtyping.

Schema evolution and versioning

Another common case of polymorphism is when documents have different shapes within the same collection, due to the progressive evolution of the document schema over time. This could be done implicitly, or with an explicit version number as part of the root-level fields of the document.

Developers love the fact that schema evolution is easy with MarkLogic. You can add or remove fields, change data types, modify indexing options, etc., to accommodate new or changing requirements without the headaches such changes would imply with relational databases.

The schema versioning pattern is described in detail later in this book. For now, it is enough to know that this pattern leverages the polymorphic capabilities of the document model.

We should manage schema evolution and versioning carefully to avoid technical debt and to consider that data may be read by different applications and SQL or BI tools that cannot handle polymorphism. Schema migration is a best practice in successful projects and organizations leveraging NoSQL, and, therefore, should be part of the schema evolution strategy to mitigate the drawbacks. We will examine more detailed approaches for schema versioning with MarkLogic in the *Design* chapter.

CHAPTER 4

About Data Models

This chapter is all about making that store-built brownie. We present the data modeling principles and concepts within a single chapter. In addition to explaining the data model, this chapter covers the three modeling characteristics of precise, minimal, and visual; the three model components of entities, relationships, and attributes; the three model levels of conceptual (align), logical (refine), and physical (design); and the three modeling perspectives of relational, dimensional, and query. By the end of this chapter, you will know how to approach any data modeling assignment.

Data model explanation

A model is a precise representation of a landscape. Precise means there is only one way to read a model—it is not ambiguous nor up to interpretation. You and I read the same model the exact same way, making the model an extremely valuable communication tool.

We need to 'speak' a language before we can discuss content. That is, once we know how to read the symbols on a model (syntax), we can discuss what the symbols represent (semantics).

Once we understand the syntax, we can discuss the semantics.

For example, a map like the one in Figure 4.1 helps a visitor navigate a city.

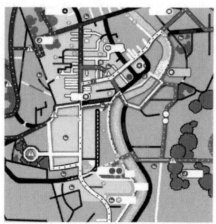

Figure 4.1: Map of a geographic landscape.

Once we know what the symbols mean on a map, such as lines representing streets, we can read the map and use it as a valuable navigation tool for understanding a geographical landscape.

A blueprint like the one in Figure 4.2 helps an architect communicate building plans. The blueprint, too, contains only representations, such as rectangles for rooms and lines for pipes. Once we know what the rectangles and lines mean on a blueprint, we know what the structure will look like and can understand the architectural landscape.

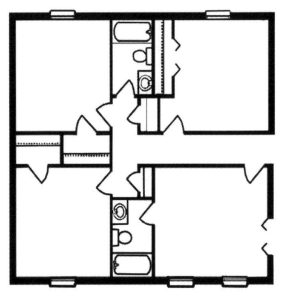

Figure 4.2: Map of an architectural landscape.

The data model, like the one in Figure 4.3, helps business professionals and technologists discuss requirements and terminology. The data model, too, contains only representations, such as rectangles for terms and lines for business rules. Once we know what the rectangles and lines mean on a data model, we can debate and eventually agree on the business requirements and terminology captured in the informational landscape.

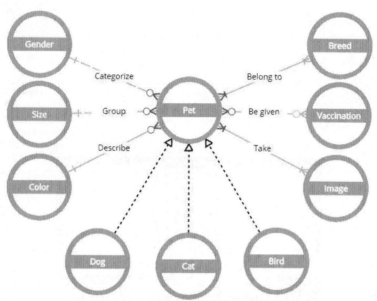

Figure 4.3: Map of an informational landscape.

A data model is a precise representation of an information landscape. We build data models to confirm and document our understanding of other perspectives.

In addition to precision, two other important characteristics of the model are minimal and visual. Let's discuss all three characteristics.

Three model characteristics

Models are valuable because they are precise—there is only one way to interpret the symbols on the model. We must transform the ambiguity in our verbal and sometimes written communication into a precise language. Precision does not mean complex—we need to keep our language simple and show the minimal amount needed for successful communication. In addition, following the maxim, *a picture is worth a thousand words*, we need visuals to communicate this precise and simple language for the initiative.

Precise, minimal, and visual are three essential characteristics of the model.

Precise

Bob: How's your course going?

Mary: Going well. But my students are complaining about too much homework. They tell me they have many other classes.

Bob: The attendees in my advanced session say the same thing.

> *Mary: I wouldn't expect that from graduates. Anyway, how many other offerings are you teaching this semester?*

> *Bob: I'm teaching five offerings this term and one is an evening not-for-credit class.*

We can let this conversation continue for a few pages, but do you see the ambiguity caused by this simple dialog?

- What is the difference between **Course**, **Class**, **Offering**, and **Session**?
- Are **Semester** and **Term** the same?
- Are **Student** and **Attendee** the same?

Precision means *exactly or sharply defined or stated.* Precision means there is only one interpretation for a term, including the term's name, definition, and connections to other terms. Most issues organizations face related to growth, credibility, and saving lives stem from a lack of precision.

On a recent project, Steve needed to explain data modeling to a group of senior human resource executives. These very high-level managers lead departments responsible for implementing a very expensive global employee expense system. Steve felt the last thing these busy human resource executives needed was a lecture on data modeling. So, instead, he asked each of these managers sitting around this large boardroom table to write down their definition of an employee. After a few minutes, most of the writing stopped and he asked them to share their definitions of an employee.

As expected, no two definitions were the same. For example, one manager included contingency workers in his definition, while another included summer interns. Instead of spending the remaining meeting time attempting to come to a consensus on the meaning of an employee, we discussed the reasons we create data models, including the value of precision. Steve explained that after we complete the difficult journey of achieving the agreed-upon employee definition and document it in the form of a data model, no one will ever have to go through the same painful process again. Instead, they can use and build upon the existing model, adding even more value for the organization.

Making terms precise is hard work. We need to transform the ambiguity in our verbal and sometimes written communication into a form where five people can read about the term and each gets a single clear picture of the term, not five different interpretations. For example, a group of business users initially define **Product** as:

Something we produce intending to sell for profit.

Is this definition precise? If you and I read this definition, are we each clear on what *something* means?

Is *something* tangible like a hammer or instead some type of service? If it is a hammer and we donate this hammer to a not-for-profit organization, is it still a hammer? After all, we didn't make a *profit* on it. The word *intending* may cover us, but still, shouldn't this word be explained in more detail? And who is *we*? Is it our entire organization or maybe just a subset? What does *profit* really mean anyway? Can two people read the word *profit* and see it very differently?

You see the problem. We need to think like detectives to find gaps and ambiguous statements in the text and make terms precise. After some debate, we update our **Product** definition to:

A product, also known as a finished product, is something that is in a state to be sold to a consumer. It has completed manufacturing, contains a wrapper, and is labeled for resale. A product is different than a raw material and a semi-finished good. A raw material, such as sugar or milk, and a semi-finished good, such as melted chocolate, are never sold to a consumer. If, in the future, sugar or milk is sold directly to consumers, then sugar and milk will become products.

Examples:
Widgets Dark Chocolate 42 oz
Lemonizer 10 oz
Blueberry pickle juice 24 oz

Ask at least five people to see if they are all clear on this particular initiative's definition of a product. The best way to test precision is to try to break the definition. Think of lots of examples and see if everyone makes the same decision as to whether the examples are products or not.

In 1967, G.H. Mealy wrote a white paper where he made this statement:

> We do not, it seems, have a very clear and commonly agreed upon set of notions about data—either what they are, how they should be fed and cared for, or their relation to the design of programming languages and operating systems.[10]

Although Mr. Mealy made this claim over 50 years ago, if we replace *programming languages and operating systems* with the word *databases*, we can make a similar claim today.

Aiming for precision can help us better understand our business terms and business requirements.

Minimal

The world around us is full of obstacles that can overwhelm our senses, making it very challenging to focus only on the relevant information needed to make intelligent decisions. Therefore, the model contains a

---

[10] G. H. Mealy, "Another Look at Data," AFIPS, pp. 525-534, 1967 Proceedings of the Fall Joint Computer Conference, 1967.
http://tw.rpi.edu/media/2013/11/11/134fa/GHMealy-1967-FJCC-p525.pdf.

minimal set of symbols and text, simplifying a subset of the real world by only including representations of what we need to understand. Much is filtered out on a model, creating an incomplete but extremely useful reflection of reality. For example, we might need to communicate descriptive information about **Customer**, such as their name, birth date, and email address. But we will not include information on the process of adding or deleting a customer.

Visuals

Visuals mean that we need a picture instead of lots of text. Our brains process images 60,000 times faster than text, and 90 percent of the information transmitted to the brain is visual.[11]

We might read an entire document but not reach that moment of clarity until we see a figure or picture summarizing everything. Imagine reading directions to navigate from one city to another versus the ease of reading a map that shows visually how the roads connect.

Three model components

The three components of a data model are entities, relationships, and attributes (including keys).

---

[11] https://www.t-sciences.com/news/humans-process-visual-data-better.

Entities

An entity is a collection of information about something important to the business. It is a noun considered basic and critical to your audience for a particular initiative. Basic means this entity is mentioned frequently in conversations while discussing the initiative. Critical means the initiative would be very different or non-existent without this entity.

The majority of entities are easy to identify and include nouns that are common across industries, such as **Customer**, **Employee**, and **Product**. Entities can have different names and meanings within departments, organizations, or industries based on audience and initiative (scope). An airline may call a **Customer** a *Passenger*, a hospital may call a **Customer** a *Patient*, and an insurance company may call a **Customer** a *Policyholder*, yet they are all recipients of goods or services.

Each entity fits into one of six categories: who, what, when, where, why, or how. That is, each entity is either a who, what, when, where, why, or how. Table 4.1 contains a definition of each of these categories, along with examples.

Category	Definition	Examples
Who	Person or organization of interest to the initiative.	Employee, Patient, Player, Suspect, Customer, Vendor, Student, Passenger, Competitor, Author
What	Product or service of interest to the initiative. What the organization makes or provides that keeps it in business.	Product, Service, Raw Material, Finished Good, Course, Song, Photograph, Tax Preparation, Policy, Breed
When	Calendar or time interval of interest to the initiative.	Schedule, Semester, Fiscal Period, Duration
Where	Location of interest to the initiative. Location can refer to actual places as well as electronic places.	Employee Home Address, Distribution Point, Customer Website
Why	Event or transaction of interest to the initiative.	Order, Return, Complaint, Withdrawal, Payment, Trade, Claim
How	Documentation of the event of interest to the initiative. Records events such as a Purchase Order (a *How*) recording an Order event (a *Why*). A document provides evidence that an event took place.	Invoice, Contract, Agreement, Purchase Order, Speeding Ticket, Packing Slip, Trade Confirmation

Table 4.1: Entity categories plus examples.

Entities are traditionally shown as rectangles on a data model, such as these two for our animal shelter:

Figure 4.4: Traditional entities.

Entity instances are the occurrences, examples, or representatives of that entity. The entity **Pet** may have multiple instances, such as Spot, Daisy, and Misty. The entity **Breed** may have multiple instances, such as German Shephard, Greyhound, and Beagle.

Entities and entity instances take on more precise names when discussing specific technologies. For example, entities are tables and instances are rows in a RDBMS like Oracle. Entities in MarkLogic align with the definition provided here, while entity instances are represented by documents.

Relationships

A relationship represents a business connection between two entities and appears on the model traditionally as a line connecting two rectangles. For example, here is a relationship between **Pet** and **Breed**:

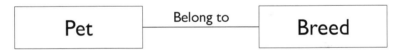

Figure 4.5: Relationship and label.

The phrase **Belong to** is called a *label*. A label adds meaning to the relationship. Instead of just saying that a **Pet** may relate to a **Breed**, we can say that a **Pet** may belong to a **Breed**. **Belong to** is more meaningful than **Relate**.

So far, we know that a relationship represents a business connection between two entities. It would be nice to know more about the relationship, such as whether a **Pet** may belong to more than one **Breed** or whether a **Breed** can categorize more than one **Pet**. Enter cardinality.

Cardinality means the additional symbols on the relationship line that communicate how many instances from one entity participate in the relationship with instances of the other entity.

There are several modeling notations, each with its own set of symbols. Throughout this book, we use a notation called *Information Engineering (IE)*. The IE notation has been a very popular notation since the early 1980s. If you use a notation other than IE within your organization, you must translate the following symbols into the corresponding symbols in your modeling notation.

We can choose any combination of zero, one, or many for cardinality. *Many* (some people use *more*) means one or more. Yes, many includes one. Specifying one or many allows us to capture *how many* of a particular entity instance participate in a given relationship. Specifying zero or one allows us to capture whether an entity instance is or is not required in a relationship.

Recall this relationship between **Pet** and **Breed**:

Figure 4.6: Relationship and label.

Let's now add cardinality.

We first ask the *Participation* questions to learn more. Participation questions tell us whether the relationship is 'one' or 'many.' So, for example:

- Can a **Pet** belong to more than one **Breed**?
- Can a **Breed** categorize more than one **Pet**?

A simple spreadsheet can keep track of these questions and their answers:

Question	Yes	No
Can a Pet belong to more than one Breed?		
Can a Breed categorize more than one Pet?		

We asked the animal shelter experts and received these answers:

Question	Yes	No
Can a Pet belong to more than one Breed?	✓	
Can a Breed categorize more than one Pet?	✓	

We learn that a **Pet** may belong to more than one **Breed**. For example, Daisy is part Beagle and part Terrier. We also learned that a **Breed** may categorize more than one **Pet**. Both Sparky and Spot are Greyhounds.

'Many' (meaning one or more) on a data model in the IE notation is a symbol that looks like a crow's foot (and is called a *crow's foot* by data folks). See Figure 4.7.

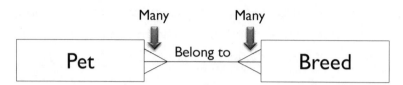

Figure 4.7: Displaying the answers to the Participation questions.

Now we know more about the relationship:

- Each **Pet** may belong to many **Breeds**.
- Each **Breed** may categorize many **Pets**.

We also always use the word 'each' when reading a relationship and start with the entity that makes the most sense to the reader, usually the one with the clearest relationship label.

This relationship is not yet precise, though. So, in addition to asking these two Participation questions, we also need to ask the *Existence* questions. Existence tells us for each relationship whether one entity can exist without the other entity. For example:

- Can a **Pet** exist without a **Breed**?
- Can a **Breed** exist without a **Pet**?

We asked the animal shelter experts and received these answers:

Question	Yes	No
Can a Pet exist without a Breed?		✓
Can a Breed exist without a Pet?	✓	

So, we learn that a **Pet** cannot exist without a **Breed**, and that a **Breed** can exist without a **Pet**. This means, for example, that we may not have any Chihuahuas in our animal shelter. Yet we need to capture a **Breed** (and in this case, one or more **Breeds**), for every **Pet**. As soon as we know about Daisy, we need to identify at least one of her breeds, such as Beagle or Terrier.

Figure 4.8 displays the answers to these two questions.

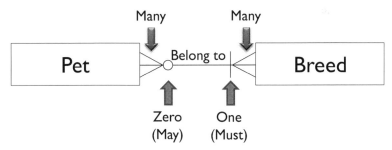

Figure 4.8: Displaying the answers to the Existence questions.

After adding existence, we have a precise relationship:

- Each **Pet** must belong to many **Breeds**.
- Each **Breed** may categorize many **Pets**.

The Existence questions are also known as the May/Must questions. The Existence questions tell us when reading the relationship, whether we say *may* or *must*. A zero means *may*, indicating optionality—the entity can exist without the other entity. A **Breed** *may* exist without a **Pet**, for example. A one means *must*, indicating required—the entity cannot exist without the other entity. A **Pet** *must* belong to at least one **Breed**, for example.

We need to ask two more questions if we are working on the more detailed logical data model (which will be discussed shortly). These are the *Identification* questions.

Identification tells us for each relationship whether one entity can be identified without the other term. For example:

- Can a **Pet** be identified without a **Breed**?
- Can a **Breed** be identified without a **Pet**?

We asked the animal shelter experts and received these answers:

Question	Yes	No
Can a Pet be identified without a Breed?	✓	
Can a Breed be identified without a Pet?	✓	

So, we learn that a **Pet** can be identified without knowing a **Breed**. We can identify the pet Sparky without knowing that Sparky is a German Shepherd. In addition, we can identify a **Breed** without knowing the **Pet**. This means, for example, that we can identify the Chihuahua breed without including any information from **Pet**.

A dotted line captures a non-identifying relationship. That is, when the answer to both questions is *yes*. A solid line captures an identifying relationship. That is, when one of the answers is *no*.

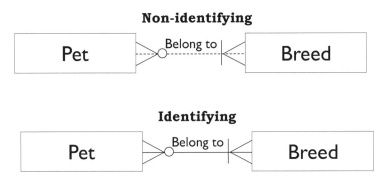

Figure 4.9: A non-identifying (top) and identifying (bottom) relationship.

So, to summarize, the Participation questions reveal whether each entity has a *one* or *many* relationship to the other entity. The Existence questions reveal whether each entity has an optional (*may*) or mandatory (*must*) relationship to the other entity. The Identification questions reveal whether each entity requires the other entity to bring back a unique entity instance.

Use instances to make things clear in the beginning and eventually help you explain your models to colleagues. See Figure 4.10 for an example.

You can see from this dataset that a **Pet** can belong to more than one **Breed**, such as Maggie being a German Shepherd/Greyhound mix. You can also see that every **Pet** must belong to at least one **Breed**. We could also have a **Breed** that is not categorizing any **Pets**, such as Chihuahua. In addition, a **Breed** can categorize multiple **Pets**, such as Joe, Jeff, and Sparky are all Beagles.

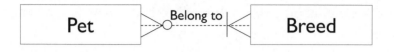

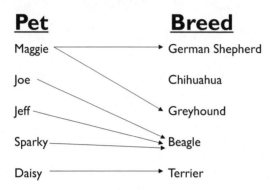

Figure 4.10: Use sample data to validate a relationship.

Answering all six questions leads to a precise relationship. Precise means we all read the model the same exact way.

Let's say that we have slightly different answers to our six questions:

Question	Yes	No
Can a Pet belong to more than one Breed?		✓
Can a Breed categorize more than one Pet?	✓	
Can a Pet exist without a Breed?		✓
Can a Breed exist without a Pet?	✓	
Can a Pet be identified without a Breed?	✓	
Can a Breed be identified without a Pet?	✓	

These six answers lead to this model:

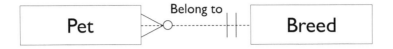

- Each **Pet** must belong to one **Breed**.
- Each **Breed** may categorize many **Pets**.

Figure 4.11: Different answers to the six questions lead to different cardinality.

In this model, we only include pure-breed pets, as a **Pet** must be assigned one **Breed**. No mutts in our shelter!

Be very clear on labels. Labels are the verbs that connect our entities (nouns). To read any complete sentence, we need both nouns and verbs. Make sure the labels on the relationship lines are as descriptive as possible. Here are some examples of good labels:

- Contain
- Provide
- Own
- Initiate
- Characterize

Avoid the following words as labels, as they provide no additional information. You can use these words in combination with other words to make a meaningful label; just avoid using these words by themselves:

- Have
- Associate

- Participate
- Relate
- Are

For example, replace the relationship sentence:

"Each **Pet** must *relate to* one **Breed**."

With:

"Each **Pet** must *belong to* one **Breed**."

Relationships take on more precise names when discussing specific technologies. For example, relationships are constraints in a RDBMS such as Oracle. Relationships in MarkLogic can be represented with references, but they are not enforceable constraints. It is often preferred to implement relationships through embedding. The pros and cons of both approaches are discussed at length later in the book.

In addition to relationship lines, we can also have a subtyping relationship. The subtyping relationship groups common entities together. For example, the **Dog** and **Cat** entities might be grouped using subtyping under the more generic **Pet** term. In this example, **Pet** would be called the grouping entity or supertype, and **Dog** and **Cat** would be the terms that are grouped together, also known as the subtypes, as shown in Figure 4.12.

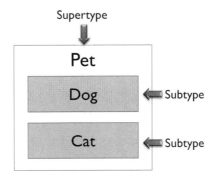

Figure 4.12: Subtyping is similar to the concept of inheritance.

We would read this model as:

- Each **Pet** may be either a **Dog** or a **Cat**.
- **Dog** is a **Pet**. **Cat** is a **Pet**.

The subtyping relationship means that all of the relationships (and attributes which we'll learn about shortly) that belong to the supertype from other terms also belong to each subtype. Therefore, the relationships to **Pet** also belong to **Dog** and **Cat**. So, for example, cats can be assigned breeds as well, so the relationship to **Breed** can exist at the **Pet** level instead of the **Dog** level, encompassing both cats and dogs. See Figure 4.13.

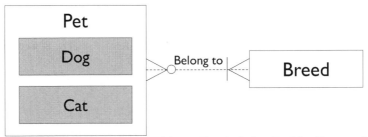

Figure 4.13: The relationship to Pet is inherited by Dog and Cat.

So, the relationship:

- Each **Pet** must belong to many **Breeds**.
- Each **Breed** may categorize many **Pets**.

Also applies to **Dog** and **Cat**:

- Each **Dog** must belong to many **Breeds**.
- Each **Breed** may categorize many **Dogs**.
- Each **Cat** must belong to many **Breeds**.
- Each **Breed** may categorize many **Cats**.

Not only does subtyping reduce redundancy, but it also makes it easier to communicate similarities across what would appear to be distinct and separate terms.

Attributes and keys

An entity contains attributes. An *attribute* is an individual piece of information whose values identify, describe, or measure instances of an entity. The entity **Pet** might contain the attributes **Pet Number** that identifies the **Pet**, **Pet Name** that describes the **Pet**, and **Pet Age** that measures the **Pet.**

Attributes take on more precise names when discussing specific technologies. For example, attributes are columns in a RDBMS such as Oracle. Attributes are fields in MarkLogic.

A candidate key is one or more attributes that uniquely identify an entity instance. We assign an **ISBN** (International Standard Book Number) to every title. The

ISBN uniquely identifies each title and is, therefore, the title's candidate key. **Tax ID** can be a candidate key for an organization in some countries, such as the United States. **Account Code** can be a candidate key for an account. A **VIN** (Vehicle Identification Number) identifies a vehicle.

A candidate key must be unique and mandatory. Unique means a candidate key value must not identify more than one entity instance (or one real-world thing). Mandatory means a candidate key cannot be empty (also known as *nullable*). Each entity instance must be identified by exactly one candidate key value.

The number of distinct values of a candidate key always equals the number of distinct entity instances. If the entity **Title** has **ISBN** as its candidate key, and if there are 500 title instances, there will also be 500 unique ISBNs.

Even though an entity may contain more than one candidate key, we can only select one candidate key to be the primary key for an entity. A primary key is the candidate key chosen as *the preferred* unique identifier for an entity. An alternate key is a candidate key that, although it has the properties of being unique and mandatory, was not chosen as the primary key. However, we can still use an alternate key to find specific entity instances.

The primary key appears above the line in the entity box, and the alternate key contains the 'AK' in parentheses. So, in the following **Pet** entity, **Pet Number** is the primary key and **Pet Name** is the alternate key. Having an alternate key on **Pet Name** means we cannot have two pets with the same name. Whether this can happen or not is a good discussion point. However, the model in its current state would not allow duplicate **Pet Names**.

Figure 4.14: An alternate key on Pet Name means we cannot have two pets with the same name.

A candidate key can be either simple, compound, or composite. If it is simple, it can be either business or surrogate. Table 4.2 contains examples of each key type.

	SIMPLE	COMPOUND	COMPOSITE	OVERLOADED
BUSINESS	ISBN	PROMOTION TYPE CODE PROMOTION START DATE	(CUSTOMER FIRST NAME + CUSTOMER LAST NAME + BIRTHDAY)	STUDENT GRADE
SURROGATE	BOOK ID			

Table 4.2: Examples of each key type.

Sometimes, a single attribute identifies an entity instance, such as **ISBN** for a title. When a single attribute makes up a key, we use the term *simple key*. A simple key can either be a business (also called natural) key or a surrogate key.

A business key is visible to the business (such as **Policy Number** for a **Policy**). A surrogate key is never visible to the business. A technologist creates a surrogate key to help with a technology issue, such as space efficiency, speed, or integration. It is a unique identifier for a table, often a counter, usually fixed-size, and always system-generated without intelligence, so a surrogate key carries no business meaning.

Sometimes it takes more than one attribute to uniquely identify an entity instance. For example, both a **Promotion Type Code** and **Promotion Start Date** may be necessary to identify a promotion. When more than one attribute makes up a key, we use the term *compound key*. Therefore, **Promotion Type Code** and **Promotion Start Date** together are a compound candidate key for a promotion. When a key contains more than one piece of information, we use the term *composite key*. A simple key that includes the customer's first name, last name, and birthday, all in the same attribute, would be an example of a simple composite key. When a key contains different attributes, it is called an *overloaded* key. A **Student Grade** attribute might sometimes contain the actual grade, such as A, B, or C. At other times, it might just contain a P for Pass and F for Fail. **Student Grade**, therefore, would be an overloaded attribute. **Student Grade** sometimes contains the student's grade, and other times indicates whether the student has passed the class.

Let's look at the model in Figure 4.15.

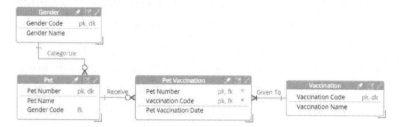

Figure 4.15: The entity on the many side contains a foreign key pointing back to the primary key from the entity on the one side.

Here are the rules captured on this model:

- Each **Gender** may categorize many **Pets**.
- Each **Pet** must be categorized by one **Gender**.
- Each **Pet** may Receive many **Vaccinations**.
- Each **Vaccination** may be given to many **Pets**.

The entity on the *one* side of the relationship is called the parent entity, and the entity on the *many* side of the relationship is called the child entity. For example, in the relationship between **Gender** and **Pet**, **Gender** is the parent and **Pet** is the child. When we create a relationship from a parent entity to a child entity, the parent's primary key is copied as a foreign key to the child. You can see the foreign key, **Gender Code**, in the **Pet** entity.

A foreign key is one or more attributes that link to another entity (or, in the case of a recursive relationship where two instances of the same entity may be related, that is, a relationship that starts and ends with the same entity, a link to the same entity). At the physical level, a foreign key allows a relational database management system to navigate from one table to another. For example, if we need to know the **Gender** of a particular **Pet**, we can use the **Gender Code** foreign key in **Pet** to navigate to the parent **Gender**.

Three model levels

Traditionally, data modeling produces a set of structures for a Relational Database Management System (RDBMS). First, we build the Conceptual Data Model (CDM) (more appropriately called the Business Terms Model or BTM for short) to capture the common business language for the initiative (e.g., *What's a Customer?*). Next, we create the Logical Data Model (LDM) using the BTM's common business language to precisely define the business requirements (e.g., *I need to see the customer's name and address on this report.*). Finally, in the Physical Data Model (PDM), we design these business requirements specific for a particular technology such as Oracle, Teradata, or SQL Server (e.g., *Customer Last Name is a variable length not null field with a non-unique index...*). Our PDM represents the RDBMS design for an application. We then generate the Data Definition Language (DDL) from the PDM, which we can run within a RDBMS environment to create the set of tables that will store the application's data. To summarize, we go from common business language to business requirements to design to tables.

Although the conceptual, logical, and physical data models have played a very important role in application development over the last 50 years, they will play an even more important role over the next 50 years.

Regardless of the technology, data complexity, or breadth of requirements, there will always be a need for a diagram that captures the business language (conceptual), the business requirements (logical), and the design (physical). However, the names conceptual, logical, and physical are deeply rooted in the RDBMS side. Therefore, we need more encompassing names to accommodate both RDBMS and NoSQL for all three levels.

- *Align = Conceptual*
- *Refine = Logical*
- *Design = Physical*

Using the terms Align, Refine, and Design instead of Conceptual, Logical, and Physical has two benefits: greater purpose and broader context.

Greater purpose means that by rebranding into Align, Refine, and Design, we include what the level does in the name. Align is about agreeing on the common business vocabulary so everyone is *aligned* on terminology and general initiative scope. Refine is about capturing the business requirements. That is, refining our knowledge of the initiative to focus on what is important. Design is about the technical requirements. That is, making sure we accommodate the unique needs of software and hardware in our model.

Broader context means there is more than just the models. When we use terms such as conceptual, most project teams only see the model as the deliverable, and do not recognize all of the work that went into producing the model or other related deliverables such as definitions, issue/question resolutions, and lineage (lineage meaning where the data comes from). The align phase includes the conceptual (business terms) model, the refine phase includes the logical model, and the design phase includes the physical model. We don't lose our modeling terms. Instead, we distinguish the model from its broader phase. For example, instead of saying we are in the logical data modeling phase, we say we are in the refine phase, where the logical data model is one of the deliverables. The logical data model exists within the context of the broader refine phase. However, if you are working with a group of stakeholders who may not warm up to the traditional names of conceptual, logical, and physical, you can call the conceptual the *alignment model*, the logical the *refinement model*, and the physical the *design model*. Use the terms that would have the largest positive impact on your audience.

The conceptual level is Align, the logical Refine, and the physical Design. Align, Refine, and Design—easy to remember and even rhymes!

Business terms (Align)

We have had many experiences where people who need to speak a common business language do not consistently use the same set of terms. For example, Steve recently facilitated a discussion between a senior business analyst and a senior manager at a large insurance company.

The senior manager expressed his frustration on how a business analyst was slowing down the development of his business analytics application. Almost word for word, this is what he said: "The team was meeting with the product owner and business users to complete the user stories on insurance quotes for our upcoming analytics application on quotes, when a business analyst asked, *What is a quote?* The rest of the meeting was wasted on trying to answer this question. Why couldn't we just focus on getting the Quote Analytics requirements, which we were in that meeting to do? We are supposed to be Agile!"

If there was a lengthy discussion trying to clarify the meaning of a quote, there is a good chance this insurance company does not understand a quote well. All business users may agree that a quote is an estimate for a policy premium but disagree at what point an estimate becomes a quote. For example, does an estimate have to be based on a certain percentage of facts before it can be considered a quote?

How well will Quote Analytics meet the user requirements if the users are not clear as to what a *quote* is? Imagine needing to know the answer to this question:

How many life insurance quotes were written last quarter in the northeast?

Without a common alignment and understanding of *quote*, one user can answer this question based on their definition of *quote*, and someone else can answer based on their different definition of *quote*. One of these users (or possibly both) will most likely get the wrong answer.

Steve worked with a university whose employees could not agree on what a *student* meant, a manufacturing company whose sales and accounting departments differed on the meaning of *return on total assets*, and a financial company whose analysts battled relentlessly over the meaning of a *trade*—it's all the same challenge we need to overcome, isn't it?

It's about working towards a common business language. A common business language is a prerequisite for success in any initiative. We can capture and communicate the terms underlying business processes and requirements, enabling people with different backgrounds and roles to understand and communicate with each other.

A Conceptual Data Model (CDM), more appropriately called a Business Terms Model (BTM), is a language of symbols and text that simplifies an informational landscape by providing a precise, minimal, and visual tool scoped for a particular initiative and tailored for a particular audience.

This definition includes the need to be well-scoped, precise, minimal, and visual. Knowing the type of visual that will have the greatest effectiveness requires knowing the audience for the model.

The audience includes the people who will validate and use the model. Validate means telling us whether the model is correct or needs adjustments. Use means reading and benefiting from the model. The scope encompasses an initiative, such as an application development project or a business intelligence program.

Knowing the audience and scope helps us decide which terms to model, what the terms mean, how the terms relate to each other, and the most beneficial type of visual. Additionally, knowing the scope ensures we don't *boil the ocean* and model every possible term in the enterprise. Instead, only focus on those that will add value to our current initiative.

Although this model is traditionally called a *conceptual data model*, the term *conceptual* is often not received as a very positive term by those outside the data field. *Conceptual* sounds like a term the IT team would come up with. Therefore, we prefer to call the *conceptual data model* the *business terms model* and will use this term going forward. It is about business terms, and including the term *business* raises its importance as a business-focused deliverable and aligns with data governance.

A business terms model often fits nicely on a single piece of paper—and not a plotter-size paper! Limiting a BTM to one page is important because it encourages us to select only key terms. We can fit 20 terms on one page but not 500 terms.

Being well-scoped, precise, minimal, and visual, the BTM provides a common business language. As a result, we can capture and communicate complex and encompassing business processes and requirements, enabling people with different backgrounds and roles to initially discuss and debate terms, and to eventually communicate effectively using these terms.

With more and more data being created and used, combined with intense competition, strict regulations, and rapid-spread social media, the financial, liability, and credibility stakes have never been higher. Therefore, the need for a common business language has never been greater. For example, Figure 4.16 contains a BTM for our animal shelter.

Each of these entities will have a precise and clear definition. For example, **Pet** might have a similar definition to what appears in Wikipedia:

A pet, or companion animal, is an animal kept primarily for a person's company or entertainment rather than as a working animal, livestock, or a laboratory animal.

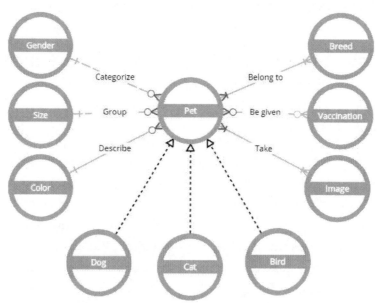

Figure 4.16: A business terms model for our animal shelter.

More than likely, though, there will be something about the definition that provides more meaning to the reader of a particular data model and is more specific to a particular initiative, such as:

A pet is a dog, cat, or bird that has passed all the exams required to secure adoption. For example, if Sparky has passed all of his physical and behavioral exams, we would consider Sparky a pet. However, if Sparky has failed at least one exam, we will label Sparky an animal that we will reevaluate later.

Let's now walk through the relationships:

- Each Pet may be either a Dog, Cat, or Bird.
- Dog is a Pet.
- Cat is a Pet.
- Bird is a Pet.
- Each Gender may categorize many Pets.
- Each Pet must be categorized by one Gender.
- Each Size may group many Pets.
- Each Pet must be grouped by one Size.
- Each Color may describe many Pets.
- Each Pet must be described by one Color.
- Each Pet must belong to many Breeds.
- Each Breed may categorize many Pets.
- Each Pet may be given many Vaccinations.
- Each Vaccination may be given to many Pets.
- Each Pet must take many Images.
- Each Image must be taken of many Pets.

Logical (Refine)

A logical data model (LDM) is a business solution to a business problem. It is how the modeler refines the business requirements without complicating the model with implementation concerns such as software and hardware. For example, after capturing the common business language for a new order application on a BTM, the LDM will refine this model with attributes and more detailed relationships and entities to capture the requirements for this order application. The BTM would contain definitions for **Order** and **Customer**, and the

LDM would contain the **Order** and **Customer** attributes needed to deliver the requirements.

Returning to our animal shelter example, Figure 4.17 contains a subset of the logical data model for our animal shelter. The requirements for our shelter application appear on this model. This model shows the attributes and relationships needed to deliver a solution to the business. For example, in the **Pet** entity, each **Pet** is identified by a **Pet Number** and described by its name and gender. **Gender** and **Vaccination** are defined lists. We also capture that a **Pet** must have one **Gender** and can receive any number (including zero) of **Vaccinations**.

Figure 4.17: Logical data model subset for our animal shelter.

Note that an LDM in the context of relational databases respects the rules of normalization. Hence, in the above diagram, there are associative entities, also known as *junction tables,* which prepare for the physical implementation of many-to-many relationships.

Since MarkLogic allows us to embed and denormalize, we often don't need these *junction tables* and opt for a simpler view of the same business rules. We can keep together what belongs together, following the Domain-Driven Design concept of *aggregates* discussed below, and leveraging denormalization. See Figure 4.18.

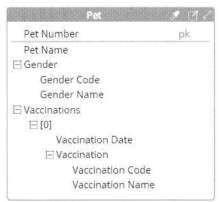

Figure 4.18: This denormalized representation can easily lead to a normalized physical data model, whereas the opposite is not necessarily true in more complex configurations.

An important part of the requirements-gathering exercise is identifying, quantifying, and qualifying the workload by recording the frequency of queries, latency of results, volume and velocity of data, data retention, etc. We'll talk more about this in the Refine chapter.

Domain-Driven Data Modeling

It is useful at this stage to discuss data modeling methodology, given that it has sometimes been accused of being in the way of getting things done. As stated in the Agile Manifesto's history page[12]: *We embrace*

---

[12] https://agilemanifesto.org/history.html.

modeling, but not in order to file some diagram in a dusty corporate repository. We've all seen ER (Entity Relationship) diagrams so big that no one understands them anymore or dares to touch them in fear of breaking them. To address this concern, Hackolade has found inspiration in a popular software development methodology called *Domain-Driven Design* and applied some of its principles to data modeling.

Eric Evans is the author of the book, *Domain-Driven Design: Tackling Complexity in the Heart of Software*, published in 2003, which is considered one of the most influential works on Domain-Driven Design (DDD).

The principles of Domain-Driven Data Modeling[13] (DDDM) include:

- **Ubiquitous language**: establishing a common language used by all project stakeholders and reflecting the concepts and terms relevant to the business. A BTM helps build a common vocabulary. DDDM pushes further for developers to use this language in the code and in the name of collections/tables and fields/columns.

- **Bounded context**: managing the complexity of the system by breaking it down into smaller, more manageable pieces. This is done by defining a boundary around each specific domain of the system. Each bounded context

---

[13] https://hackolade.com/dddm.html.

has its own model and language that is appropriate for that context.

- **Focus on the core domain:** concentrating efforts for maximum impact on what matters most, without letting scope creep, and while leveraging pre-existing conformed dimensions and generic concepts.

- **Reach a shared understanding**: collaborating with subject matter experts in the business to ensure alignment on the context and meaning of data.

- **Aggregates**: identifying clusters of related objects, and treating each of them as a single unit of change. Aggregates help to enforce consistency and integrity within a domain.

- **Continuous refinement**: an iterative process with continuous refinement of the domain model as new insights and requirements are discovered. The domain model should evolve and improve over time based on feedback from stakeholders and users.

Some data modeling traditionalists have expressed reservations about DDD (and also about Agile development.) For every methodology and technology, there are, of course, examples of misinterpretation and misguided efforts. However, if applied with clairvoyance and experience, DDDM and Agile lead to great success.

DDDM is particularly relevant in the context of NoSQL databases and modern architecture patterns, including event-driven[14] and micro-services[15]. Specifically, the DDDM concept of *aggregate* objects and denormalization. As a result, the strict definition of a logical data model is too constraining as it implies that the technology-agnostic model respects the rules of normalization. Hackolade has extended the capabilities of its technology-agnostic models to allow complex data types for nesting and denormalization in Polyglot data models to accommodate the support of NoSQL structures.

Physical (Design)

The physical data model (PDM) is the logical data model compromised for specific software or hardware. The BTM captures our common business vocabulary, the LDM our business requirements, and the PDM our technical requirements. That is, the PDM is a data model of our business requirements structured to work well with our technology. The physical represents the technical design.

While building the PDM, we address the issues that have to do with specific hardware or software, such as, how can we best design our structures to:

- Process this operational data as quickly as possible?
- Make this information secure?

---

[14] https://en.wikipedia.org/wiki/Event-driven_architecture.

[15] https://en.wikipedia.org/wiki/Microservices.

- Answer these business questions with a sub-second response?

For example, Figure 4.19 contains a relational version and Figure 4.20 a nested version of a subset of the physical data model for our animal shelter:

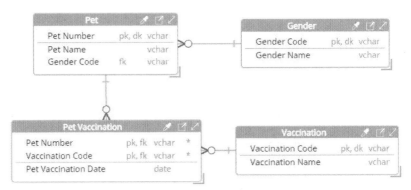

Figure 4.19: Relational physical data models for our animal shelter.

Pet			
Pet URI	pk	str
Pet Name		str
⊟ Gender		obj
Gender Code		str
Gender Name		str
⊟ Vaccinations		arr
⊟ [0]		obj
Vaccination Date		str
⊟ Vaccination		obj
Vaccination Code		str
Vaccination Name		str

Figure 4.20: Nested physical data models for our animal shelter.

In the physical data model, we have compromised our logical model to work with specific technology. For example, if we are implementing in a RDBMS such as Oracle, we might need to combine (denormalize) structures together to make retrieval performance acceptable.

Figure 4.19 is a normalized RDBMS model and Figure 4.20 shows one possible denormalization that leverages MarkLogic's document approach. Information belonging together is kept together with the nesting of subobjects. The cardinality of the relational junction table Pet Vaccination is replaced by an array to store multiple Vaccinations. This aggregation approach enables the referential integrity of the atomic unit of each document. Note that the nesting does not prevent the existence of a Vaccination table if an access pattern in the application requires it, but it would then require synchronization of the denormalized data to ensure consistency.

Three model perspectives

Relational Database Management System (RDBMS) and NoSQL are the two main modeling perspectives. Within the RDBMS, the two settings are relational and dimensional. Within NoSQL, the one setting is query. Therefore, the three modeling perspectives are relational, dimensional, and query.

Table 4.3 contrasts relational, dimensional, and query. In this section, we will go into more detail into each of these perspectives.

A RDBMS stores data in sets based on Ted Codd's groundbreaking white papers written from 1969 through 1974. Codd's ideas were implemented in the RDBMS with tables (entities at the physical level) containing attributes. Each table has a primary key and foreign key constraints to enforce the relationships between tables.

Factor	Relational	Dimensional	Query
Benefit	Precisely representing data through sets	Precisely representing how data will be analyzed	Precisely representing how data will be received and accessed
Focus	Business rules *constraining* a business process	Business questions *analyzing* a business process	Access paths *providing insights* into a business process
Use case	Operational (OLTP)	Analytics (OLAP)	Discovery
Parent perspective	RDBMS	RDBMS	NoSQL
Example	A Customer must own at least one Account.	How much revenue did we generate in fees by Date, Region, and Product? Also want to see by Month and Year...	Which customers own a checking account that generated over $10,000 in fees this year, own at least one cat, and live within 500 miles of New York City?

Table 4.3: Comparing relational, dimensional, and query.

The RDBMS has been around for so many years primarily because of its ability to retain data integrity by enforcing rules that maintain high-quality data.

Secondly, the RDBMS enables efficiency in storing data, reducing redundancy, and saving storage space at the cost of using more CPU power. Over the last decade, the benefit of saving space has diminished as disks get cheaper while CPU performance is not improving. Both trajectories favor NoSQL databases these days.

Relational, dimensional, and query can exist at all three model levels, giving us nine different types of models, as shown in Table 4.4. We discussed the three levels of Align, Refine, and Design in the previous section. We align on a common business language, refine our business requirements, and then design our database. For example, if we are modeling a new claims application for an insurance company, we might create a relational model capturing the business rules within the claims process. The BTM would capture the claims business vocabulary, the LDM would capture the claims business requirements, and the PDM would capture the claims database design.

	RELATIONAL	DIMENSIONAL	NoSQL
BUSINESS TERMS (ALIGN)	TERMS AND RULES	TERMS AND PATHS	TERMS AND QUERIES
LOGICAL (REFINE)	SETS	MEASURES WITH CONTEXT	QUERY-FOCUSED HIERACHY
PHYSICAL (DESIGN)	COMPROMISED SETS	STAR SCHEMA OR SNOWFLAKE	ENHANCED HIERACHY

Table 4.4: Nine different types of models.

Relational

Relational models work best when there is a requirement to capture and enforce business rules. For example, a relational model may be ideal if an operational application requires applying many business rules, such as an order application ensuring that every order line belongs to one and only one order, and that each order line is identified by its order number plus a sequence number. The relational perspective focuses on business rules.

We can build a relational model at all three levels: business terms, logical, and physical. The relational business terms model contains the common business language for a particular initiative. Relationships capture the business rules between these terms. The relational logical data model includes entities along with their definitions, relationships, and attributes. The relational physical data model includes physical structures such as tables, columns, and constraints. The business terms, logical, and physical data models shared earlier are relational. See Figures 4.21, 4.22, and 4.23.

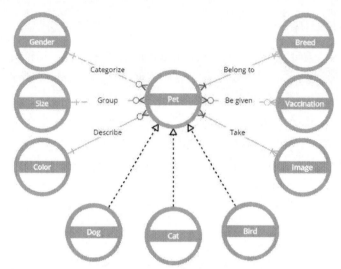

Figure 4.21: Relational BTM.

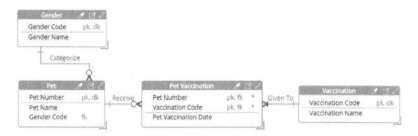

Figure 4.22: Relational LDM.

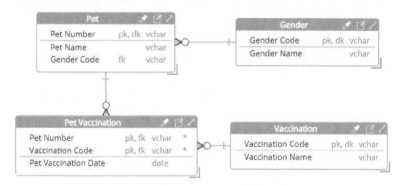

Figure 4.23 Relational PDM.

Figure 4.24 contains another example of a BTM for a banking scenario.

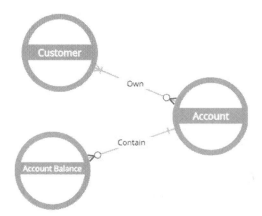

Figure 4.24: Relational BTM for a bank.

The relationships capture that:

Each **Customer** may own many **Accounts**.

Each **Account** must be owned by many **Customers**.

Each **Account** may contain many **Account Balances**.

Each **Account Balance** must belong to one **Account**.

We wrote the following definitions during one of our meetings with the project sponsor:

Customer	A customer is a person or organization who has opened one or more accounts with our bank. If members of a household each have their own account, each member of a household is considered a distinct customer. If someone has opened an account and then closed it, they are still considered a customer.

Account	An account is a contractual arrangement by which our bank holds funds on behalf of a customer.
Account Balance	An account balance is a financial record of how much money a customer has in a particular account with our bank at the end of a given time period, such as someone's checking account balance at the end of a month.

For the relational logical data model, we assign attributes to entities (sets) using a set of rules called *normalization*.

Although normalization has a foundation in mathematics (set theory and predicate calculus), we see it more as a technique to design a flexible structure. More specifically, we define normalization as a process of asking business questions, increasing your knowledge of the business and enabling you to build flexible structures that support high-quality data.

The business questions are organized around levels, including First Normal Form (1NF), Second Normal Form (2NF), and Third Normal Form (3NF). These three levels have been neatly summarized by William Kent:

Every attribute depends upon the key, the whole key, and nothing but the key, so help me Codd.

Every attribute depends upon the key is 1NF, *the whole key* is 2NF, and *nothing but the key* is 3NF. Note that the higher levels of normalization include the lower levels, so 2NF includes 1NF, and 3NF includes 2NF and 1NF.

To make sure that every attribute depends upon the key (1NF), we need to make sure for a given primary key value, we get at most one value back from each attribute. For example, **Author Name** assigned to a **Book** entity would violate 1NF because we can have more than one author for a given book, such as this book. Therefore, **Author Name** does not belong to the **Book** set (entity) and needs to be moved to a different entity. More than likely, **Author Name** will be assigned to the **Author** entity, and a relationship will exist between **Book** and **Author,** stating among other things, that a **Book** can be written by more than one **Author**.

To make sure every attribute depends upon the whole key (2NF), we need to make sure we have the minimal primary key. For example, if the primary key for **Book** was both **ISBN** and a **Book Title**, we would quickly learn that **Book Title** is not necessary to have in the primary key. An attribute such as **Book Price** would depend directly on the **ISBN,** and therefore, including **Book Title** in the primary key would not add any value.

To make sure there are no hidden dependencies (*nothing but the key*, which is 3NF), we need to make sure every attribute depends directly on the primary key and nothing else. For example, the attribute **Order Gross**

Amount does not depend directly on the primary key of **Order** (most likely, **Order Number**). Instead, **Order Gross Amount** depends upon **List Price** and **Item Quantity,** which are used to derive the **Order Gross Amount**.

Data Modeling Made Simple, by Steve Hoberman, goes into more detail about each level of normalization, including the levels above 3NF. Realize the main purpose of normalization is to correctly organize attributes into sets. Also, note that the normalized model is built according to the properties of the data and not built according to how the data is being used.

Dimensional models are built to answer specific business questions with ease, and NoSQL models are built to answer queries and identify patterns with ease. The relational model is the only model focused on the intrinsic properties of the data and not usage.

Dimensional

A dimensional data model captures the business *questions* behind one or more business processes. The answers to the questions are metrics, such as **Gross Sales Amount** and **Customer Count**.

A dimensional model is a data model whose only purpose is to allow efficient and user-friendly filtering, sorting, and summing of measures. That is, analytics applications. The relationships in a dimensional model represent navigation paths instead of business rules, as with the relational model. The scope of a dimensional model is a collection of related measures plus context that together address some business process. We build dimensional models based on one or more business questions that evaluate a business process. We parse the business questions into measures and ways of looking at these measures to create the model.

For example, suppose we work for a bank and would like to better understand the fee generation process. We might ask the business question, *What is the total amount of fees received by* **Account Type** *(such as Checking or Savings),* **Month, Customer Category** *(such as Individual or Corporate), and* **Branch?** See Figure 4.25. This model also communicates the requirement to see fees not just at a Month level but also at a Year, not just a Branch level, but also at a Region and District.

Figure 4.25: A dimensional BTM for a bank.

Term definitions:

Fee Generation	Fee generation is the business process where money is charged to customers for the privilege to conduct transactions against their account, or money charged based on time intervals, such as monthly charges to keep a checking account open with a low balance.
Branch	A branch is a physical location open for business. Customers visit branches to conduct transactions.
Region	A region is our bank's own definition of dividing a country into smaller pieces for branch assignment or reporting purposes.
District	A district is a grouping of regions used for organizational assignments or reporting purposes. Districts such as North America and Europe can and often do cross country boundaries.
Customer Category	A customer category is a grouping of one or more customers for reporting or organizational purposes. Examples of customer categories are Individual, Corporate, and Joint.
Account Type	An account type is a grouping of one or more accounts for reporting or organizational purposes. Examples of account types are Checking, Savings, and Brokerage.
Year	A year is a period of time containing 365 days, consistent with the Gregorian calendar.
Month	A month is each of the twelve named periods into which a year is divided.

You might encounter terms such as **Year** and **Month,** which are commonly understood terms, and therefore, minimal time can be invested in writing a definition. Make sure, though, that these are commonly understood terms, as sometimes even **Year** can have multiple meanings, such as whether the reference is to a fiscal or standard calendar.

Fee Generation is an example of a meter. A meter represents the business process that we need to measure. The meter is so important to the dimensional model that the name of the meter is often the name of the application: the **Sales** meter, the Sales Analytics Application. **District**, **Region**, and **Branch** represent the levels of detail we can navigate within the **Organization** dimension. A *dimension* is a subject whose purpose is to add meaning to the measures. For example, **Year** and **Month** represent the levels of detail we can navigate within the **Calendar** dimension. So this model contains four dimensions: **Organization**, **Calendar**, **Customer**, and **Account**.

Suppose an organization builds an analytical application to answer questions on how a business process is performing, such as a sales analytics application. Business questions become very important in this case, so we build a dimensional data model. The dimensional perspective focuses on business questions. We can build a dimensional data model at all three levels: business terms, logical, and physical. Figure 4.25 displays our business terms model, Figure 4.26 shows the logical, and Figure 4.27 the physical.

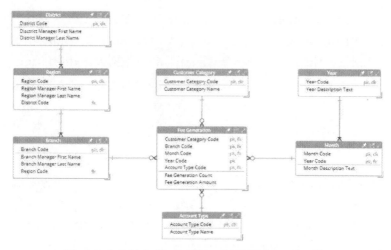

Figure 4.26: A dimensional LDM for a bank.

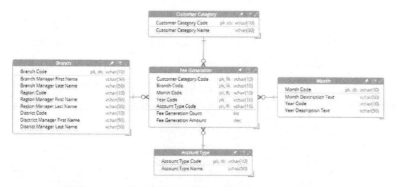

Figure 4.27: A dimensional PDM for a bank.

Query

Suppose an organization builds an application to discover something new about a business process, such as a fraud detection application. Queries become very important in that case, so we build a query data model.

We can build a query data model at all three levels: business terms, logical, and physical. Figure 4.28 contains a query business terms model, Figure 4.29 and Figure 4.30 the query logical data models, and Figure 4.31 the query physical data model.

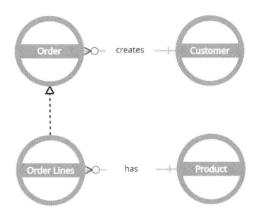

Figure 4.28: A query BTM.

The Query BTM does not look any different from other BTMs as the vocabulary and scope are the same, independent of the physical database implementation. In fact, we can even ask the Participation and Existence questions for each relationship in our query BTM, if we feel that it would add value. In the above example:

a **Customer** creates an **Order**
an **Order** is made of **Order Lines**
an **Order Line** has a **Product**

It is possible to toggle the display of attributes for the different entities.

When it comes to the logical model, however, access patterns and workload analysis dictate the model.

Depending on whether there are queries for maintenance screens for Customers and Products, you could have the strictly embedded logical model in Figure 4.29 or the model in Figure 4.30.

The first logical model would lead to a group of documents in MarkLogic, which could be minimally assigned to one collection, whereas it will be automatically normalized into three tables when instantiated to a physical model for a relational database. Recall that MarkLogic does not restrict that a document must belong to only one collection. Rather, a document can be organized in more than one collection without duplicating the data or not assigned to a collection at all.

Figure 4.29: Strictly embedded logical model.

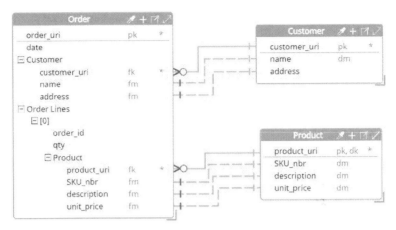

Figure 4.30: A query LDM.

The second logical model could lead to three collections in MarkLogic to accommodate the maintenance of **Customers** and **Products**, but keeping the **Order** table as an aggregate combines embedding and referencing schema design patterns. The logical model can also lead to different directories like /customers/, /products/ & /orders/. Collections and Directories are good ways to organize data for query efficiency.

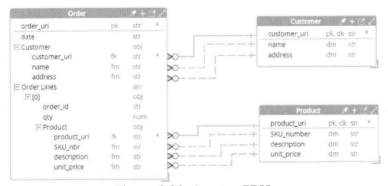

Figure 4.31: A query PDM.

In the above model, we show nesting, denormalization, and referencing. Nesting allows aggregating information that belongs together in a user-friendly structure to make it easily understandable by humans. Denormalization is implemented so a query to retrieve an order would fetch all of the necessary information in a single seek without executing expensive joins, even if it is a repetition of the data in the master collections Customer and Product. Access patterns might still be required to view and update Customer and Product information regardless of the orders to which they might be linked. Therefore, we keep the master Customer collection and the master Product collection. In the Order collection, we keep a reference to the master document. Since there is no cross-document referential integrity built into the database engine, the responsibility to maintain the synchronization shifts to the application or to an offline process such as a Kafka pub/sub pipeline.

One final remark: there could be a good reason not to update a denormalized piece of information. For example, the ship-to address of an already fulfilled order should not be updated because a customer moves to a new address. Only pending orders should be updated. Denormalization is sometimes more precise than cascading updates.

CHAPTER 5

Align

This chapter will explain the data modeling align phase. We explain the purpose of aligning our business vocabulary, introduce our animal shelter case study, and then walk through the align approach. We end this chapter with three tips and three takeaways.

Purpose

The align stage aims to capture a common business vocabulary within a business terms model for a particular initiative.

For NoSQL models, you might use a different term than a business terms model, such as a *query alignment model.* We like this term, which is specific to the purpose of a NoSQL BTM, as our goal is modeling the queries.

Our animal shelter

A small animal shelter needs our help. They currently advertise their ready-to-adopt pets on their own website. They use a Microsoft Access relational database to keep track of their animals, and publish this data weekly on their website. See Figure 5.1 for their current process.

Figure 5.1: Animal shelter current architecture.

A Microsoft Access record is created for each animal after the animal passes a series of intake tests and is deemed ready for adoption. The animal is called a pet once they are ready for adoption.

Once a week, the pet records are updated on the shelter's website. New pets are added and adopted pets have been removed. Not many people know about this shelter, and, therefore, animals often remain unadopted for much longer than the national average. Consequently, they would like to partner with a group of animal shelters to form a consortium where all of the shelters' pet information will appear on a much more popular website. Our shelter will need to extract data from its current MS Access database and send it to the consortium database in JSON format. The consortium will then load these JSON feeds into their MarkLogic database with a web front end.

Let's now look at the shelter's current models. The animal shelter built the business terms model (BTM) in Figure 5.2 to capture the common business language for the initiative. In addition to this diagram, the BTM also contains precise definitions for each term, such as this definition **Pet** mentioned earlier in the chapter:

A pet is a dog, cat, or bird that has passed all the exams required to secure adoption. For example, if Sparky has passed all of his physical and behavioral exams, we would consider Sparky a pet. However, if Sparky has failed at least one exam, we will label Sparky an animal that we will reevaluate later.

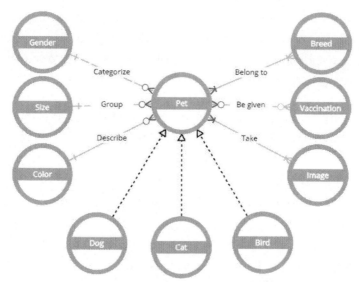

Figure 5.2: Animal shelter BTM.

Our animal shelter knows its world well and has built fairly solid models. Recall they will send a subset of their data to a consortium via JSON, which the consortium's MarkLogic database will receive and load for display on their website. Let's go through the align, refine, and design approach for the consortium, and then work on the JSON structure required to move the shelter's data from Microsoft Access to MarkLogic.

Approach

The align stage is about developing the initiative's common business vocabulary. We will follow the steps shown in Figure 5.3.

Before you begin any project, we must ask six strategic questions (Step 1). These questions are a prerequisite to the success of any initiative because they ensure we choose the right terms for our BTM. Next, identify all terms within the scope of the initiative (Step 2). Make sure each term is clearly and completely defined. Then determine how these terms are related to each other (Step 3). Often, you will need to go back to Step 2 at this point because in capturing relationships, you may come up with new terms. Next, determine the most beneficial visual for your audience (Step 4). Consider the visual that would resonate best with those needing to review and use your BTM. As a final step, seek approval of your BTM (Step 5). Often, at this point, there are additional changes to the model, and we cycle through these steps until the model is accepted.

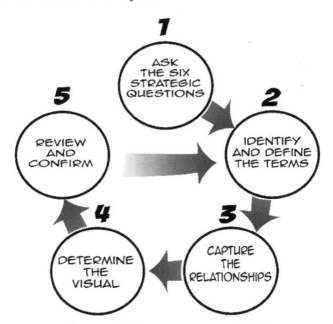

Figure 5.3: Steps to create a BTM.

Let's build a BTM following these five steps.

Step 1: Ask the six strategic questions

Six questions must be asked to ensure a valuable BTM. These questions appear in Figure 5.4.

Figure 5.4: Six questions to ensure model success.

1. **What is our initiative?** This question ensures we know enough about the initiative to determine the scope. Knowing the scope lets us decide which terms should appear on the initiative's BTM. In his book Domain-Driven Design, Eric Evans introduces the concept of *Bounded Context*, which is all about understanding and defining your scope. For example, terms such as **Animal**, **Shelter Employee**, and **Pet Food** are out of scope.

2. **Flexibility or simplicity?** This question ensures we introduce generic terms only if there is a need for flexibility. Generic terms allow us to accommodate new types of terms that we do not know about today and also allow us to better group similar terms together. For example, **Person** is flexible and **Employee** is simple. **Person** can include other terms we have not yet considered, such as **Adopter, Veterinarian**, and **Volunteer**. However, **Person** can be a more difficult term to relate to than **Employee.** We often describe our processes using business-specific terms like **Employee.**

3. **Now or later?** This question ensures we have chosen the correct time perspective for our BTM. BTMs capture a common business language at a point in time. If we are intent on capturing how business processes work or are analyzed today, then we need to make sure terms, along with their definitions and relationships, reflect a current perspective (now). If we are intent on capturing how business processes work or are analyzed at some point in the future, such as one year or three years into the future, then we need to make sure terms, along with their definitions and relationships, reflect a future perspective (later).

4. **Forward or reverse engineering?** This question ensures we select the most appropriate *language* for the BTM. If business requirements

drive the initiative, then it is a forward engineering effort and we choose a business language. It does not matter whether the organization is using SAP or Siebel, the BTM will contain business terms. If an application drives the initiative, then it is a reverse engineering effort and we choose an application language. If the application uses the term **Object** for the term **Product**, it will appear as **Object** on the model and be defined according to how the application defines the term, not how the business defines the term. As another example of reverse engineering, you might have some type of physical data structure as your starting point, such as a database layout or an XML or JSON document. For example, the following JSON snippet might reveal the importance of **Shelter Volunteer** as a business term:

```
{
  "name": "John Smith",
  "age": 35,
  "address": {
      "street": "123 Main St",
      "city": "Anytown",
      "state": "CA",
      "zip": "12345"
    }
}
```

5. **Operational, analytics, or query?** This question ensures we choose the right type of BTM— relational, dimensional, or query. Each initiative requires its respective BTM.

6. **Who is our audience?** We need to know who will review our model (validator) and who will use our model going forward (users).

1. What is our initiative?

Mary is the animal shelter volunteer responsible for intake. Intake is the process of receiving an animal and preparing the animal for adoption. She has been a volunteer for over ten years, and was the main business resource in building the original Microsoft Access database. She is enthusiastic about the new initiative, seeing it as a way to get animals adopted in less time. We might start off by interviewing Mary, where the goal is to have a clear understanding of the initiative, including its scope:

> **You**: Thanks for making time to meet with me. This is just our first meeting, and I don't want to keep you behind our allocated time, so let's get right to the purpose of our interview and then a few questions. The earlier we identify our scope and then define the terms within this scope, the greater the chance for success. Can you please share with me more about this initiative?

> **Mary**: Sure! The main driver for our initiative is to make our furry friends get adopted faster. Today, on average, our pets are adopted in two weeks. We and other small local shelters would like to get this down to five days on average. Maybe even less, hope so. We will send our pet data to a consortium we have formed with other local shelters to centralize our listings and reach a wider audience.

You: Do you have all types of pets, or just dogs and cats?

Mary: I'm not sure what kinds of pets the other shelters have other than dogs and cats, but we also have birds up for adoption.

You: Ok, and are there any pets to exclude from this initiative?

Mary: Well, it takes a few days to assess an animal to be considered ready for adoption. We run some tests and sometimes procedures. I like to use the term pet when an animal has completed these processes and is now ready for adoption. So, we do have animals that are not yet pets. We are only including pets in this initiative.

You: Got it. And when somebody is looking for a furry best friend, what kinds of filters would they use?

Mary: I've talked with volunteers at the other shelters, too. We feel after filtering first on the type of pet, such as dog, cat, or bird, filtering by breed, gender, color, and size would be the most important filters.

You: What kinds of information would someone expect to see when clicking on a pet description that was returned by the filter selections?

Mary: Lots of images, a cute name, maybe information on the pet's color or breed. That sort of thing.

You: Makes sense. What about people? Do you care about people as part of this initiative?

Mary: What do you mean?

You: Well, the people who drop off pets and the people who adopt pets.

Mary: Yes, yes. We keep track of this information. By the way, the people who drop off animals we call surrenderers, and the people who adopt pets are adopters. We are not sending any person details to the consortium. We don't see it relevant and don't want to risk getting sued over privacy issues. Spot the dog will never sue us, but Bob the surrenderer might.

You: I can understand that. Well, I think I understand the scope of the initiative, thank you.

We now have a good understanding of the scope of the initiative. It includes all pets (not all animals) and no people. As we refine the terminology, we might have more questions for Mary around scope.

2. Flexibility or simplicity?

Let's continue the interview to answer the next question.

You: Flexibility or simplicity?

Mary: I don't understand the question.

You: We need to determine whether to use generic terms or, for lack of a better word, more concrete terms. Using generic terms, such as mammal instead of **dog** or **cat,** allows us to accommodate future terms later, such as other kinds of mammals like monkeys or whales.

Mary: We haven't had many whales up for adoption this month. [laughs]

You: Ha!

Mary: Flexibility sounds appealing, but we shouldn't go overboard. I can see eventually we might have other kinds of pets, so a certain level of flexibility would be useful here. But not too much. I remember working on the Microsoft Access system and someone was trying to get us to use a Party concept to capture dogs and cats. It was too hard for us to get our heads around it. Too fuzzy if you know what I mean.

You: I do know what you mean. Ok, a little flexibility to accommodate different kinds of pets, but not to go overboard. Got it.

3. Now or later?

Now on to the next question.

You: Should our model reflect how things are now at the shelter or how you would like it to be after the consortium's application is live?

Mary: I don't think it matters. We are not changing anything with the new system. A pet is a pet.

You: Ok, that makes things easy.

As we can see from our conversations on these first three questions, getting to the answers is rarely straightforward and easy. However, it is much more efficient to ask them at the beginning of the initiative instead of making assumptions early on and performing rework later, when changes are time-consuming and expensive.

4. Forward or reverse engineering?

Since we first need to understand how the business works before implementing a software solution, this is a forward engineering project, and we will choose the forward engineering option. This means driven by requirements and, therefore, our terms will be business terms instead of application terms.

5. Operational, analytics, or query?

Since this initiative is about displaying pet information to drive pet adoption, which is query, we will build a query BTM.

6. Who is our audience?

That is, who is going to validate the model and who is going to use it going forward? Mary seems like the best candidate to be the validator. She knows the existing application and processes very well and is vested in ensuring the new initiative succeeds. Potential adopters will be the users of the system.

Step 2: Identify and define the terms

We first focus on the user stories, then determine the detailed queries for each story, and finally sequence these queries in the order they occur. It can be iterative. For example, we might identify the sequence between two queries and realize that a query in the middle is missing that will require modifying or adding a user story. Let's go through each of these three steps.

1. Write user stories

User stories have been around for a long time and are extremely useful for NoSQL modeling. Wikipedia defines a user story as: *...an informal, natural language description of features of a software system.*

The user story provides the scope and overview for the BTM, also known as a query alignment model. A query alignment model accommodates one or more user stories. The purpose of a user story is to capture at a very high level how an initiative will deliver business value. User stories take the structure of the template in Figure 5.5.

TEMPLATE	COVERS
AS A (STAKEHOLDER)	WHO?
I WANT TO (REQUIREMENT)	WHAT?
SO THAT (MOTIVATION)	WHY?

Figure 5.5: User story template.

Here are some user stories from https://tech.gsa.gov/:

- As a Content Owner, I want to be able to create product content so that I can provide information and market to customers.

- As an Editor, I want to review content before it is published so that I can ensure it is optimized with correct grammar and tone.

- As a HR Manager, I need to view a candidate's status so that I can manage their application process throughout the recruiting phases.

- As a Marketing Data Analyst, I need to run the Salesforce and Google Analytics reports so that I can build the monthly media campaign plans.

To keep our animal shelter example relatively simple, assume our animal shelter and others that are part of the consortium met and agreed on these user stories:

1. As a potential dog adopter, I want to find a particular breed, color, size, and gender, so that I get the type of dog I'm looking for. I want to ensure that the dog's vaccinations are up-to-date.

2. As a potential bird adopter, I want to find a particular breed and color so that I get the bird I'm looking for.

3. As a potential cat adopter, I want to find a particular color and gender, so that I get the type of cat I'm looking for.

2. Capture queries

Next, we capture the queries for the one or more user stories within our initiative's scope. While we want to capture multiple user stories to ensure we have a firm grasp of the scope, having just a single user story that drives a NoSQL application is ok. A query starts off with a *verb* and is an action to do something. Some NoSQL database vendors use the phrase *access pattern* instead of query. We will use the term *query* to also encompass *access pattern*.

Here are the queries that satisfy our three user stories:

Q1: Only show pets available for adoption.

Q2: Search available dogs by breed, color, size, and gender that have up-to-date vaccinations.

Q3: Search available birds by breed and color.

Q4: Search available cats by color and gender.

Now that we have direction, we can work with the business experts to identify and define the terms within the initiative's scope.

Recall our definition of a term as a noun that represents a collection of business data and is considered both basic and critical to your audience for a particular initiative. A term can fit into one of six categories: who, what, when, where, why, or how. We can use these six categories to create a terms template for capturing the terms on our BTM. See Figure 5.6.

This is a handy brainstorming tool. There is no significance to the numbers. That is, a term written next to #1 is not meant to be more important than a term written next to #2. In addition, you can have more than five terms in a given column or, in some cases, no terms in a given column.

WHO ?	WHAT ?	WHEN ?	WHERE ?	WHY ?	HOW ?

Figure 5.6: Terms template.

We meet again with Mary, and came up with this completed template in Figure 5.7, based on our queries.

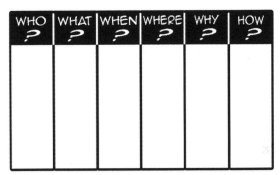

WHO ?	WHAT ?	WHEN ?	WHERE ?	WHY ?	HOW ?
SURRENDERER	PET	VACCINATION DATE	CRATE	VACCINATE	VACCINATION
ADOPTER	DOG			ADOPT	ADOPTION
	CAT			PROMOTE	PROMOTION
	BIRD				
	BREED				
	GENDER				
	COLOR				
	SIZE				
	IMAGE				

Figure 5.7: Initially completed template for our animal shelter.

Notice that this is a brainstorming session, and terms might appear on this template but not on the relational BTM. Excluded terms fit into three categories:

- **Too detailed**. Attributes will appear on the LDM and not the BTM. For example, **Vaccination Date** is more detailed than **Pet** and **Breed**.

- **Out of scope**. Brainstorming is a great way to test the scope of the initiative. Often, terms added to the terms template require additional discussions to determine whether they are in scope. For example, **Surrenderer** and **Adopter** we know are out of scope for the animal shelter's initiative.

- **Redundancies**. Why and How can be very similar. For example, the event **Vaccinate** is documented by the **Vaccination**. The event **Adopt** is documented by **Adoption**. Therefore, we may not need both the event and documentation. In this case, we choose the documentation. That is, we choose How instead of Why.

After taking a lunch break, we met again with Mary and refined our terms template, as shown in Figure 5.8.

We might have a lot of questions during this brainstorming session. It is a great idea to ask questions as they come up.

WHO ?	WHAT ?	WHEN ?	WHERE ?	WHY ?	HOW ?
~~SURRENDERER~~	PET	~~VACCINATION DATE~~	~~COAT~~	~~VACCINATE~~	VACCINATION
~~ADOPTER~~	DOG			~~ADOPT~~	~~ADOPTION~~
	CAT			~~PROMOTE~~	~~PROMOTION~~
	BIRD				
	BREED				
	GENDER				
	COLOR				
	SIZE				
	IMAGE				

Figure 5.8: Refined template for our animal shelter.

There are three benefits of raising questions:

- **Become known as the detective**. Become comfortable with the level of detective work needed to arrive at a precise set of terms. Look for holes in the definition where ambiguity can sneak in, and ask questions the answers to which will make the definition precise. Consider the question, *Can a pet be of more than one breed?* The answer to this question will refine how the consortium views pets, breeds, and their relationship. A skilled detective remains pragmatic as well, careful to avoid *analysis paralysis*. A skilled data modeler must also be pragmatic to ensure the delivery of value to the project team.

- **Uncover hidden terms**. The answers to questions often lead to more terms on our

BTM—terms that we might have missed otherwise. For example, a better understanding of the relationship between **Vaccination** and **Pet** might lead to more terms on our BTM.

- **Better now than later**. The resulting BTM offers a lot of value, yet the process of getting to that final model is also valuable. Debates and questions challenge people, make them rethink and, in some cases, defend their perspectives. If questions are not raised and answered during the process of building the BTM, the questions will be raised and need to be addressed later on in the lifecycle of the initiative, often in the form of data and process surprises, when changes are time-consuming and expensive. Even simple questions like *Are there other attributes that we could use to describe a pet?* can lead to a healthy debate, resulting in a more precise BTM.

Here are definitions for each term:

Pet	A dog, cat, or bird that is ready and available to be adopted. An animal becomes a pet after they have passed certain exams administered by our shelter staff.
Gender	The biological sex of the pet. There are three values that we use at the shelter: • Male • Female • Unknown The unknown value is when we are unsure of the gender.

Size	The size is most relevant for dogs, and there are three values that we assign at the shelter: • Small • Medium • Large Cats and birds are assigned medium, except for kittens which are assigned small and parrots which are large.
Color	The primary shade of the pet's fur, feathers, or coat. Examples of colors include brown, red, gold, cream, and black. If a pet has multiple colors, we either assign a primary color or assign a more general term to encompass multiple colors, such as textured, spotted, or patched.
Breed	From Wikipedia, because this definition applies to our initiative: *A breed is a specific group of domestic animals having homogeneous appearance, homogeneous behavior, and/or other characteristics that distinguish it from other organisms of the same species.*
Dog	From Wikipedia, because this definition applies to our initiative: *The dog is a domesticated descendant of the wolf. Also called the domestic dog, it is derived from the extinct Pleistocene wolf, and the modern wolf is the dog's nearest living relative. Dogs were the first species to be domesticated by hunter-gatherers over 15,000 years ago before the development of agriculture.*
Image	A photograph taken of the pet that will be posted on the website.

Cat	From Wikipedia, because this definition applies to our initiative:
	The cat is a domestic species of small carnivorous mammal. It is the only domesticated species in the family Felidae and is commonly referred to as the domestic cat or house cat to distinguish it from the wild members of the family.
Bird	From Wikipedia, because this definition applies to our initiative:
	Birds are a group of warm-blooded vertebrates constituting the class Aves, characterized by feathers, toothless beaked jaws, the laying of hard-shelled eggs, a high metabolic rate, a four-chambered heart, and a strong yet lightweight skeleton.
Vaccination	A shot given to a pet to protect it from disease. Examples of vaccinations are rabies for dogs and cats, and polyomavirus vaccine for birds.

Step 3: Capture the relationships

Even though this is a query BTM, we can ask the Participation and Existence questions to precisely display the business rules for each relationship. Participation questions determine whether there is a one or a many symbol on the relationship line next to each term. Existence questions determine whether there is a zero (may) or one (must) symbol on the relationship line next to either term.

Working with Mary, we identify these relationships in the model:

Pet can be a **Bird, Cat,** or **Dog.** (Subtyping)

Pet and **Image.**

Pet and **Breed.**

Pet and **Gender.**

Pet and **Color.**

Pet and **Vaccination.**

Pet and **Size.**

Table 5.1 contains the answers to the Participation and Existence questions for each of these seven relationships (excluding the subtyping relationship).

After translating the answer to each question into the model, we have the animal shelter BTM in Figure 5.9.

Question	Yes	No
Can a Gender categorize more than one Pet?	✓	
Can a Pet be categorized by more than one Gender?		✓
Can a Gender exist without a Pet?	✓	
Can a Pet exist without a Gender?		✓
Can a Size categorize more than one Pet?	✓	
Can a Pet be categorized by more than one Size?		✓
Can a Size exist without a Pet?	✓	
Can a Pet exist without a Size?		✓
Can a Color describe more than one Pet?	✓	
Can a Pet be described by more than one Color?		✓
Can a Color exist without a Pet?	✓	
Can a Pet exist without a Color?		✓

Question	Yes	No
Can a Pet be described by more than one Breed?	✓	
Can a Breed describe more than one Pet?	✓	
Can a Pet exist without a Breed?		✓
Can a Breed exist without a Pet?	✓	
Can a Pet be given more than one Vaccination?	✓	
Can a Vaccination be given to more than one Pet?	✓	
Can a Pet exist without a Vaccination?	✓	
Can a Vaccination exist without a Pet?	✓	
Can a Pet take more than one Image?	✓	
Can an Image be taken of more than one Pet?	✓	
Can a Pet exist without an Image?		✓
Can an Image exist without a Pet?		✓

Table 5.1: Answers to the Participation and Existence questions.

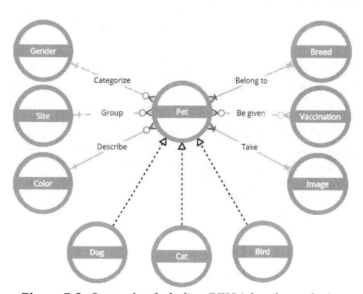

Figure 5.9: Our animal shelter BTM (showing rules).

These relationships are read as:

Each **Gender** may categorize many **Pets**.

Each **Pet** must be categorized by one **Gender**.

Each **Size** may group many **Pets**.

Each **Pet** must be grouped by one **Size**.

Each **Color** may describe many **Pets**.

Each **Pet** must be described by one **Color**.

Each **Pet** must belong to many **Breeds**.

Each **Breed** may be assigned to many **Pets**.

Each **Pet** may be given many **Vaccinations**.

Each **Vaccination** may be given to many **Pets**.

Each **Pet** must take many **Images**.

Each **Image** must be taken of many **Pets**.

Each **Pet** may either be a **Dog**, **Cat**, or **Bird**.

Dog is a **Pet**. **Cat** is a **Pet**. **Bird** is a **Pet**.

The answers to the participation and existence questions are context-dependent. That is, the scope of the initiative determines the answers. In this case, because our scope is the subset of the animal shelter's business that will be used as part of this consortium's project, we know at this point that a **Pet** must be described by only one **Color**.

We determined, though, that a MarkLogic database should be used to answer these queries. You can see how the traditional data model provides value in terms of making us ask the right questions and then providing a powerful communication medium showing the terms and their business rules. Even if we are not implementing our solution in a relational database, this BTM provides value.

Build a relational data model even though the solution is in a NoSQL database such as MarkLogic, if you feel there can be value. That is, if you feel there is value in explaining the terms with precision along with their business rules, build the relational BTM. If you feel there is value in organizing the attributes into sets using normalization, build the relational LDM. It will help you organize your thoughts and provide you with a very effective communication tool.

Our end goal, though, is to create a MarkLogic database. Therefore, we need a query BTM. So, we need to determine the order in which someone would run the queries. Graphing the sequence of queries leads to the query BTM. The query BTM is a numbered list of all queries necessary to deliver the user stories within the initiative's scope. The model also shows a sequence or dependency among the queries. The query BTM for our five queries would look like what appears in Figure 5.10.

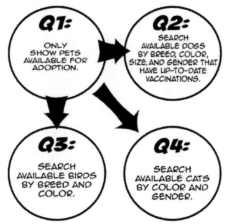

Figure 5.10: Our animal shelter BTM (showing queries).

All of the queries depend on the first query. That is, we first need to filter by animal type.

Step 4: Determine the visual

Someone will need to review your work and use your model as input for future deliverables such as software development, so deciding on the most useful visual is an important step. After getting an answer to Strategic Question #4, *Who is our audience?*, we know that Mary will be our validator.

There are many different ways of displaying the BTM. Factors include the technical competence of the audience and the existing tools environment.

However, it would be helpful to know which data modeling notations and data modeling tools are currently being used within the organization. If the audience is familiar with a particular data modeling notation—such as Information Engineering (IE), which we have been using throughout this book—that is the notation we should use. If the audience is familiar with a particular data modeling tool, such as IDERA's ER/Studio, erwin DM, or Hackolade Studio, and that data modeling tool uses a different notation, we should use that tool with that notation to create the BTM.

Luckily, the two BTMs we created, one for rules and one for queries, are very intuitive, so there is a very good chance our models will be well-understood by the audience.

Step 5: Review and confirm

Previously, we identified the person or group responsible for validating the model. Now, we need to show them the model and make sure it is correct. Often, after reviewing the model at this stage, we make some changes and then show them the model again. This iterative cycle continues until the validator approves the model.

Three tips

1. **Organization**. The steps you went through in building this *model* are the same steps we go through in building any model. It is all about organizing information. Data modelers are fantastic organizers. We take the chaotic real world and show it in a precise form, creating powerful communication tools.

3. **80/20 Rule.** Don't go for perfection. Too many requirements meetings end with unfulfilled goals by spending too much time discussing a minute particular issue. After a few minutes of discussion, if you feel the issue's discussion may take up too much time and not lead to a resolution, document the issue and keep going. You will find that for modeling to work well with Agile and other iterative approaches, you may have to forego perfection and sometimes even completion. Much better to document the unanswered questions and issues and keep going. Much better to deliver something imperfect yet still very valuable than deliver nothing. You will find that you can get the data

model about 80% complete in 20% of the time. One of your deliverables will be a document containing unanswered questions and unresolved issues. Once all of these issues and questions are resolved, which will take about 80% of your time to complete, the model will be 100% complete.

4. **Diplomat.** As William Kent said in **Data and Reality** (1978), *so, once again, if we are going to have a database about books, before we can know what one representative stands for, we had better have a consensus among all users as to what "one book" is.* Invest time trying to get consensus on terms before building a solution. Imagine someone querying on pets without having a clear definition of what a pet is.

Three takeaways

1. Six strategic questions must be asked before you begin any project (Step 1). These questions are a prerequisite to the success of any initiative because they ensure we choose the right terms for our BTM. Next, identify all terms within the scope of the initiative (Step 2). Make sure each term is clearly and completely defined. Then, determine how these terms are related (Step 3). Often, you will need to go back to Step 2 at this point because in capturing relationships, you may come up with new terms. Next, determine the most beneficial visual for your audience (Step 4). Consider the visual that would resonate best with those needing to review and

use your BTM. As a final step, seek approval of your BTM (Step 5). At this point, there are often additional changes to the model, and we cycle through these steps until the model is accepted.

5. Create a relational BTM in addition to a query BTM if you feel there would be value in capturing and explaining the participation and existence rules.

6. Never underestimate the value of precise and complete definitions.

CHAPTER 6

Refine

This chapter will explain the data modeling refine phase. We explain the purpose of refine, refine the model for our animal shelter case study, and then walk through the refine approach. We end the chapter with three tips and three takeaways.

Purpose

The purpose of the refinement stage is to create the logical data model (LDM) based on our common business vocabulary defined during the align stage. Refine is how the modeler captures the business requirements without complicating the model with implementation concerns, such as software and hardware.

The shelter's Logical Data Model (LDM) uses the common business language from the BTM to precisely define the business requirements. The LDM is fully-attributed yet independent of technology. We build the relational LDM by normalizing, covered in Chapter 4. Figure 6.1 contains the shelter's relational LDM.

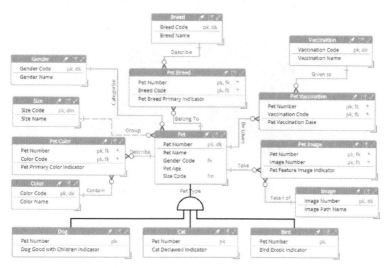

Figure 6.1: Animal shelter relational LDM.

This model does not change based on requirements. Therefore, we can use it as the starting point model for all queries. Let's briefly walk through the model. The shelter identifies each **Pet** with a **Pet Number**, which is a unique counter assigned to the **Pet** the day the **Pet** arrives. Also entered at this time are the pet's name (**Pet Name**) and age (**Pet Age**). If the **Pet** does not have a name, it is given one by the shelter employee entering the pet's information. If the age is unknown, it is estimated by the shelter employee entering the pet's information. If the **Pet** is a **Dog**, the shelter employee entering the information performs a few assessments to determine whether the Dog is good with children (**Dog Good With Children Indicator**). If the **Pet** is a **Cat**, the shelter employee determines whether the **Cat** has been declawed (**Cat Declawed Indicator**). If the Pet is a **Bird**, the shelter employee enters whether it is an exotic bird such as a parrot (**Bird Exotic Indicator**).

Approach

The refine stage is all about determining the business requirements for the initiative. The end goal is a logical data model which captures the attributes and relationships needed to answer the queries. The steps to complete appear in Figure 6.2.

Similar to determining the more detailed structures in a traditional logical data model, we determine the more detailed structures needed to deliver the queries during the refinement stage. You can, therefore, call the query LDM a query refinement model if you prefer. The query refinement model is all about discovery and captures the answers to the queries that reveal insights into a business process.

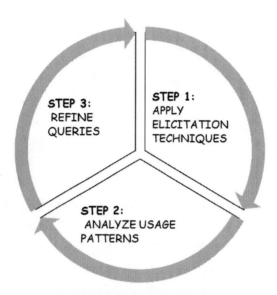

Figure 6.2: Refinement steps.

Step 1: Apply elicitation techniques

Let us visit the realm of business application development. Today, modern applications are predominantly developed using object-oriented programming languages such as Java, JavaScript, Python, and C#. Studies indicate that software development has become more accessible to a broader audience (aka, democratized), with JavaScript, Python, and Java retaining their leading positions in popularity for a decade. Data structures in these programming languages are treated as *objects,* each possessing attributes and methods. However, when the database data model operates differently, such as in a relational database management system (RDBMS), it creates what is known as an "impedance mismatch." This mismatch arises when there's a disparity between how data is handled in the database and in the application programming.

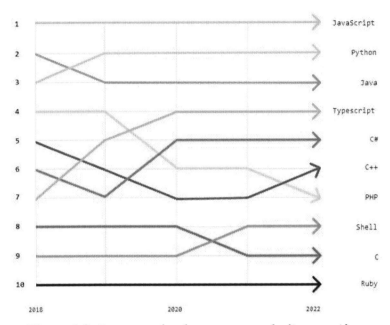

Figure 6.3: Programming language popularity over time.

To mitigate this impedance mismatch, developers employ a technique called "object-relational mapping" (ORM), which establishes a bi-directional mapping between objects in the application layer and the data represented in the RDBMS schema. Essentially, this means that while the database is optimized for storage, the interaction with business stakeholders occurs at the application layer, where business data is represented differently. This approach often results in lengthy development cycles, performance issues, and buggy code due to the challenges in transferring requirements between application and database developers.

NoSQL databases like MarkLogic provide a robust alternative to this dilemma. With a document database, developers utilize a "flexible data model" that aligns more seamlessly with modern application development, effectively sidestepping the impedance mismatch problem. The document model empowers developers to maintain data integrity across all tiers of the application stack.

Layer	Technology	Data Model	Execution
Front End	Angular ReactJS VueJS Streamlite	JSON	
		Mapping	
Middle Tier	Node.js Java Python C#	JavaScript	Full stack JavaScript Development
		ORM	
Database	MarkLogic	JSON	

Figure 6.4: Maintaining data integrity across the application stack.

Although not the main focus of this book, the intention of this explanation is to emphasize the importance of involving database developers in elicitation techniques. It involves the collaboration of data modelers, database developers, and business stakeholders to identify the entities, attributes, and relationships necessary to address queries from business applications. Various techniques are traditionally employed in this collaboration, including interviews, analysis of business requirement documents and data mapping documents, and observation of current business processes. These techniques can be combined in different ways and are adaptable to various software development methodologies such as Agile or Waterfall.

However, there are instances where business stakeholders struggle to articulate their needs effectively. In such cases, alternative techniques may need to be explored. One such effective technique is to build prototypes, allowing business stakeholders to visualize and better communicate their requirements. This approach facilitates clearer communication and ensures the resulting solutions more accurately meet the needs of the business.

For a database, workload analysis is the process of systematically examining the patterns, characteristics, and demands placed by its users or components. The goal of workload analysis is to gain insights into how the system is utilized in real-world scenarios, including the types and frequencies of operations performed, resource consumption patterns, performance metrics, and potential scalability and security considerations.

A properly configured MarkLogic database can scale to petabytes of data and thousands of transactions per second. This requires analyzing workloads to understand how data is generated and used. This analysis is essential for optimizing MarkLogic to handle large data volumes and high transaction loads effectively.

Measure Connections

A key piece of information to gather from business stakeholders and ensure is effectively communicated to the design process involves the relationships between entities. Let's take the example of customers, orders, and products. Customers place orders, and orders consist of products. If customer data includes orders and order data includes products, the size of customer documents will balloon over time, possibly exceeding the recommended document size for MarkLogic. The ideal document size in MarkLogic is 100K +/- two orders of magnitude. Initially, embedding entities may seem appealing because accessing a customer document provides a comprehensive overview of that customer (often referred to as a 360-degree view). However, with time, the process of querying and updating customer documents will gradually slow down (larger documents take longer to retrieve and will consume more memory), leading to the realization that referencing could have been a preferable approach over embedding. Therefore, it's crucial to determine the scale of 'many' in one-to-many relationships and the potential number of such relationships for an entity. While achieving perfect accuracy in measurement from the outset may pose challenges, obtaining a solid estimate of the maximum, minimum, and average connections between entities will aid in optimizing data modeling.

Step 2: Analyze Usage Patterns

What is the end goal? A web application, an analytics application, or both? Imagine a web application that allows searching for customers and can navigate down to orders and products. Getting a million customers to the webpage together is never a good idea. But getting 20 customers at a time with a pagination option is a better user experience. Also, for all 20 customers, getting all orders and products together is not a good idea. A better way would be to list the customers, and clicking on a customer shows the orders, and clicking on order shows the products. Then, we have smaller and more targeted queries.

The strategy mentioned above is well-suited for interactive applications. However, in the case of a machine learning platform or a data warehouse, it's necessary to analyze all documents together. The continuous synchronization of millions of customer, order, and product records to these systems can be quite time-consuming and inefficient. Incorporating a "last_update_dt" field in each entity can significantly expedite synchronization. By doing so, only records updated within the last 'N' minutes need to be synchronized. With proper indexing based on the "last_update_dt" field, the entire system can achieve high performance and resource efficiency.

There are several additional usage-related questions that can be addressed early on. For instance, determining whether the system should support wildcard searches or identifying which facets *(groupings of records based on indexed terms or value ranges)* should be available for applying search filters. Obtaining early answers to these questions can facilitate the proper configuration of the system in terms of indexes and resource allocation, ensuring efficient performance and alignment with user needs.

Step 3: Refine Queries

It's a fact: the best database query isn't crafted in the initial attempt. Queries should undergo iterative profiling and testing to reach their optimal performance level. Return only the data required. Developers tend to return entire documents regardless of whether all the data in the document is required. In modern multi-tier architectures, this can have performance implications, especially when processing many documents.

Like other databases, MarkLogic comes equipped with query profiling tools that offer insights into index usage, query costs, and other valuable details for fine-tuning queries. During testing and profiling, several key considerations should be kept in mind.

1. **Ensure testing and profiling occur on a system with a comparable data volume and configuration to the production environment**. A query that performs well on a smaller dataset

may not exhibit the same efficiency when dealing with millions of records. Extrapolating results from a smaller environment can lead to inaccuracies.

2. **Utilize realistic data during testing**. For instance, if all customer records share the same date of birth, querying for that date may cause system hang-ups. Thus, generating test data with a realistic distribution is crucial for accurately assessing query efficiency.

3. **Conduct tests in isolation and under various conditions**. While testing queries in isolation is necessary, it's equally vital to assess performance alongside other business processes. For example, the query's performance when no updates are occurring versus when thousands of updates are happening

4. **Manage business expectations**. Establish Service Level Agreements (SLAs) by engaging with business stakeholders to define performance expectations for queries. These SLAs serve as benchmarks for validating the system's performance. Any deviation from the agreed-upon SLAs may necessitate refining the queries or revisiting the SLAs with the business stakeholders. This iterative process ensures that the system's performance aligns with the business requirements and expectations.

Three tips

1. **Usage patterns:** the query-driven approach is critical to leverage the benefits of NoSQL when creating an LDM. Don't be tempted by old normalization habits unless the workload analysis reveals relationship cardinality that warrants normalization.

2. **Aggregates:** keep together what belongs together! A nested structure in a single document can ensure atomicity and consistency of inserts, updates, and queries without expensive joins. It is also beneficial for developers who are used to working with objects, and it is easier to understand for humans.

3. **Choose between Normalized and Denormalized data:** Careful consideration between normalization and denormalization is crucial in data modeling. When the facts gathered during the elicitation process are applied to modeling, it may become evident that maintaining relationships through denormalized data is more advantageous than normalization. It's essential to recognize that while denormalization can improve query performance and simplify data access, it may lead to redundancy and potential data integrity issues. However, it's also important to keep in mind that it's generally easier to normalize a denormalized model than the reverse. Therefore, striking the right balance between normalization and

denormalization based on the specific requirements of the system is key. This ensures optimal performance, data integrity, and scalability while allowing for flexibility in adapting to future changes in the data model.

Three takeaways

1. The purpose of the refinement stage is to create the logical data model (LDM) based on our common business vocabulary, defined for our initiative during the align stage. Refine is how the modeler captures the business requirements without complicating the model with implementation concerns, such as software and hardware.

2. An LDM is typically fully-attributed yet independent of technology. But this strict definition is being challenged nowadays with the fact that technology targets can be so different in nature: relational databases, the different families of NoSQL, storage formats for data lakes, pub/sub pipelines, APIs, etc.

3. It used to be, with relational databases, that you wanted to design a structure that could handle any possible future query that might be run down the road. With NoSQL, you want to design schemas that are specific, not only for an application, but for each access pattern (write or read) in that application.

CHAPTER 7

Design

This chapter will explain the data modeling design phase. We explain the purpose of design, design the model for our animal shelter case study, and then walk through the design approach. We end the chapter with three tips and three takeaways.

Purpose

The purpose of the design stage is to create the physical data model (PDM) based on the business requirements defined in our logical data model. Design is how the modeler captures the technical requirements without compromising the business requirements, yet accommodating the initiative's software and technology needs used for the initiative.

The design stage is also where we accommodate history. That is, we modify our structures to capture how data changes over time. For example, the design stage would allow us to keep track of not just the most recent name for a pet, but also the original. For example, the animal shelter changes a pet's name from Sparky to Daisy. Our design could store the original pet name and the most current, so we would know Daisy's original name was Sparky. Although this is not a book on temporal data or modeling approaches that gracefully allow for storing high data volatility or varying history requirements, such as the Data Vault[16], you would need to consider such factors in the Design stage.

Figure 7.1 shows the Physical Data Model (PDM) of the animal shelter's Microsoft Access database design.

Note that the PDM includes formatting and nullability. Also, this model is heavily denormalized. For example:

---

[16] For more on the data vault, read John Giles' *The Elephant in the Fridge*.

Although the logical communicates that a **Pet** can have any number of images, their design only allows up to three images for each **Pet**. The shelter uses **Image_Path_Name_1** for the featured image.

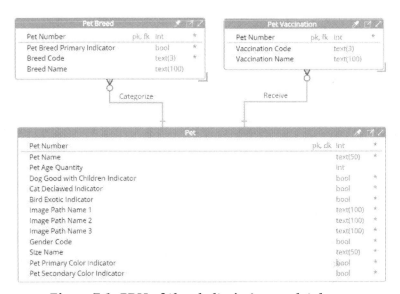

Figure 7.1: PDM of the shelter's Access database.

Notice how the decode entities from the logical have been addressed. The one-to-many relationships are denormalized into **Pet**. **Gender_Name** is not needed because everyone knows the codes. People are not familiar with **Size_Code** so only **Size_Name** is stored. **Breed** has been denormalized into **Pet_Breed**. It is common for decode entities to be modeled in different ways on the physical, depending on the requirements.

Vaccination has been denormalized into **Pet_Vaccination**.

For MarkLogic, it would look more like the model in Figure 7.2.

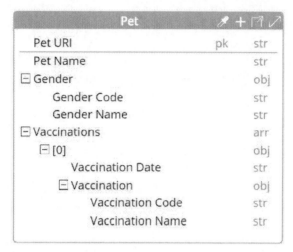

Figure 7.2: If modeling the shelter's Access database in MarkLogic.

Approach

The design stage is all about developing the database-specific design for the initiative. The end goal is the query PDM, which we can also call the *query design model*. For our animal shelter initiative, this model captures the MarkLogic design and JSON interchange format. The steps to complete appear in Figure 7.3.

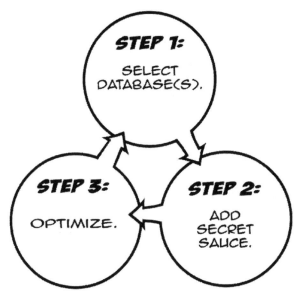

Figure 7.3: Design steps.

Step 1: Select database(s)

We now know enough to decide which database would be ideal for the application. Sometimes, we might choose multiple databases if we feel it would be the best architecture for the application. We know the consortium uses JSON for transport and MarkLogic for storage.

Step 2: Add secret sauce

Although document NoSQL databases can be quite similar, each database has something special to consider during design. For example, for MarkLogic, we would consider where to use their secret sauce, such as MarkLogic-specific functionality like the following:

- Indexes
- Collections and URIs for use in query/search and document organization
- Document versioning and temporality
- Document relationships with semantic triples
- Read and write concerns

MarkLogic schema design principles

Here are some basic principles when modeling document schemas for MarkLogic.

1. **Data design focus:** Build human-oriented intuitive models that are readable and understandable by non-technical users. For example, if you show a recipe JSON document to someone, he or she will easily see that the root object name labels it as a recipe, that the recipe has ingredients and steps, and so on.

2. **Use Query-Driven approach:** Also referred to as *model by access*, using a query-driven design. Start by documenting the types of queries your application will perform most frequently, along with the data the queries return, and design your schema/documents to support those queries efficiently. If your end-users search for books and authors, those are good candidates for high-level document types in your database.

3. **Denormalization (cardinality):** One-to-one and one-to-many relationships should be included in documents to the extent possible. Many-to-many relationships should use documents of each type with cross-document linking

performed with unique document URIs that are either stored in the documents themselves or stored as a collection name on the referenced (linked) documents. These unique IDs should be indexed with *range indexes* to allow for fast joins between the different types of documents. Alternatively, we can leverage RDF relations here. The next section, *Embedding versus Referencing*, provides additional perspectives.

4. **Data duplication**: Sometimes, you want to replicate some basic elements (e.g., dates and names) from one document type to another to perform queries without doing joins. For instance, a book document might include an author's name (for quick searches or faceting) and an ID (to retrieve additional information), but not the author's birthdate, home location, etc.

5. **Flattened data versus structured hierarchy:** While we discussed benefits of grouping data with hierarchical subobjects in *The JSON Document Model* chapter, JSON properties should be flattened and not arbitrarily grouped (nested) for convenience. Nesting introduces dependence on the parent object for semantic meaning of the data property. In addition, MarkLogic indexing is more efficient when JSON property names are unique in the database. The use of naming standards such as the ISO/IEC 11179-5[17] facilitate consistent data naming and meaning. In some cases, such as a collection of

---

[17] https://www.iso.org/standard/60341.html

properties representing a single structure, it may make sense to keep the structured hierarchy such as in the *customer* object in Figure 3.5. You should carefully consider these cases and use nesting if they make semantic sense.

For example, we can represent an address in two ways, as shown in the example below. While the structured way is probably more appealing visually, there is no semantic benefit from it. Is address really an object or is the grouping for visualization only? Since there is only one address, the address properties are simple attributes, and thus, introducing an address object changes nothing semantically. Avoiding unnecessary groupings also reduces the work required to transform or "flatten" a JSON/XML schema to non-hierarchical targets such as a data warehouse. The structured method can lengthen query strings by the introduction of additional node(s), such as the "address" object.

Flattened Address:

```
{
    "company": "ACME",
    "website": "https://www.acme.com/",
    "addressLine1": "111 Main",
    "addressLine2": "3rd Floor",
    "state": "NY",
    "city": "New York",
    "zip": "10011"
}
```

Structured Address:

```
{
  "company": "ACME",
  "website": "https://www.acme.com/",
  "address": {
    "line1": "111 Main",
    "line2": "3rd Floor",
    "state": "NY",
    "city": "New York",
    "zip": "10011"
  }
}
```

Additional considerations

1. Recall earlier that a document (entity) is a collection of information about something important to the business. At the physical design layer, you can think of designing a document, like designing a table. Individual instances of a document are like rows in the table.

2. Unlike the fixed rows of a table, documents are like very flexible rows that contain built-in relationships. As the above principles mention, take advantage of as many embedded relationships as possible. There are two primary reasons to consider:

   a. Lock contention situations can be reduced as MarkLogic locks are at the document level.

   b. Indexing, retrieval, and updates happen at the document level.

7. Consider the document size when deciding what to include in a single document:

    a. The ideal document size ranges from 1K to 100K.

    b. Sizes larger than 100K are acceptable depending on hardware infrastructure and response time needs. Sizes smaller than 1K are associated with more overhead.

8. Since MarkLogic normally updates documents by writing a completely new document to the database and invalidating the older version, as long as documents are adhering to the above size constraints, the frequency of updates of individual elements should not be a major consideration in partitioning documents unless the frequency of updates is very high.

9. In MarkLogic, documents are ACID-compliant for cluster-wide updates.

10. Collections are much more flexible than tables. Remember, in MarkLogic, a document can be in multiple collections simultaneously. We can use collections for fast searches and joins across disparate documents.

11. MarkLogic indexes cannot be scoped at the collection or directory level. Therefore, if you want to restrict indexes to certain documents or collections, there are two options:

    a. Model the data with separate property/element names or use

namespaces for XML documents.
Reference item *Flattened data versus
structured hierarchy* in prior list.

    b. Use Path Range or Field Range indexes as
long as the path to the document
property name is unique across
document types.

12. Accommodate lineage information (who, when,
why, and what) in the model, even if the
business use case does not demand it. Such
use cases will evolve like below:

    a. Change Data Capture (CDC) or replicate
data to another system

    b. Purge or archive data based on a
condition.

    c. Leverage storage optimization (Tiered
Storage)

    d. Insights into outliers, such as documents
updated several times a day when the
average update frequency is only a couple
of times.

13. Since models change and evolve, include a
version identifier as metadata or as part of the
document to help in model change management
as well as validating documents against a model.

14. Always include a root object in the JSON
document that serves to identify the document
type (i.e., the entity). This approach is preferred
over a property embedded somewhere in the

document that may not be as easily seen. Identifying the type is also useful in collections consisting of multiple document types.

```
{
    "order": {
        "orderNumber": 123910,
        "lastName": "Cruise",
        "firstName": "Tom"
        }
}
                        verses
{
    "orderNumber": 123910,
    "docType": "order",
    "lastName": "Cruise",
    "firstName": "Tom"
}
```

a. As MarkLogic stores both JSON and XML in a tree structure, having a root is beneficial for things like XQuery and certain MarkLogic functions.

b. A document represents some entity, such as a *Pet*, for example, and thus, it makes logical sense to expect a *Pet* object and not a generic object that has a property with *Pet* for value. This approach also aligns with object oriented programming languages where an *object* or *class* has a name to identify type, as shown below.

```
public class Pet {
  int id;
  String name;

  public static void main(String args[]) {
    Pet p1 = new Pet();
    p1.id = 1001;
    p1.name = "Moose";
    System.out.println(p1.id);
    System.out.println(p1.name);
  }
}
```

Embedding versus referencing

How far do I go with de-normalization in my document design? We have already encouraged that one-to-many relationships be embedded in the document. Choosing whether to embed or reference a relationship will lead to a different solution in each case. Making the right decision for each relationship will give you the best model among all possible models.

Embedding

In a relational database model, one-to-one relationships tend to be embedded. The two pieces of information live in the same row. In the case of one-to-many or many-to-many relationships, the two pieces of information are divided into different rows in different tables. With MarkLogic, embedding a one-to-one relationship means putting the two pieces of data in the same document. You could also opt to use subobjects to group related information, such as the components of an address:

```
// A one-to-one relationship within a subobject
{
  "docUri": "/pet/dog/dog19370824",
   "petName": "Champ",
  "petOwner": {
     "Name": "President of the United States",
     "street": "1600 Pennsylvania Avenue NW",
     "city": "Washington",
     "state": "DC",
     "zip": "20500",
     "country": "USA"
   }
}
```

You embed a one-to-many relationship with an array. An array is the document construct to express a one-to-many relationship in the document model.

```
// a Pet document with embedded Pet comments
{
  "docUri": "/pet/dog/dog28261913",
  "petName": "Fanny",
  "comments": [ {
     "name": "Sandy Davis",
     "text": "Fanny is the sweetest dog ever!"
   }, {
     "name": "Steve Hoberman",
     "text": "Fanny loved my daughter's brownies."
   }
  ]
}
```

For a many-to-many relationship, we also use an array. It is important to note that embedding this type of relationship may introduce data duplication. Data duplication is not necessarily bad for your model. However, we want to highlight the difference between embedding a one-to-many relationship, which does not introduce denormalization or data duplication, with a many-to-many relationship.

Referencing

We reference another document by using a scalar if the relationship is a *one* or with an array of *references* if the relationship is a *many*. References can be unidirectional or bi-directional. We can use the document identifier, the document URI in the case of MarkLogic, to reference the other document. MarkLogic does not mandate that the reference be a document URI. We can use any properly indexed JSON property, and this may be preferable if there are multiple keys to produce the correct reference.

```
{
  "docUri": "/pet/comment/dog/comment101",
  "dogId": "28261913",
  "name": "Sandy Davis",
  "text": "Fanny is the sweetest dog ever!"
}
```

Using the example of **Pet** and related comments, we can describe the relationship as: *A Pet may have many comments* and *A comment must be associated with a Pet*. The following examples show the different ways we can model this relationship. Example of references from the parent's document:

```
// References from the parent document to the child
// documents using an array
//
// a Pet document with references to Comment
// documents
{
  "docUri": "/pet/dog/dog28261913",
  "name": "Fanny",
  "comments": [
    "/pet/comment/dog/comment101",
    "/pet/comment/dog/comment102"
  ]
}
// referenced Comment documents
{
  "docUri": "/pet/comment/dog/comment101",
  "name": "Sandy Davis",
  "text": "Fanny is the sweetest dog ever!"
}
{
  "docUri": "/pet/comment/dog/comment102",
  "name": "Steve Hoberman",
  "text": "Fanny loved my daughter's brownies."
}
```

Examples of references from the children's documents:

```
// References from a child document to the parent
// document
//
// a Pet document
{
  "docUri": "/pet/dog/dog28261913",
  "name": "Fanny"
}
```

```
// Comment documents with reference to the parent
document
{
  "docUri": "/pet/comment/dog/comment101",
  "dogUri": "/pet/dog/dog28261913",
  "name": "Sandy Davis",
  "text": "Fanny is the sweetest dog ever!"
}
{
  "docUri": "/pet/comment/dog/comment102",
  "dogUri": "/pet/dog/dog28261913",
  "name": "Steve Hoberman",
  "text": "Fanny loved my daughter's brownies."
}
```

Example of bi-directional references:

```
// References from the parent document to the child
// documents and vice-versa
//
// a Pet document with references to Comment
// documents
{
  "docUri": "/pet/comment/dog/comment101",
  "name": "Fanny",
  "comments": [
      "/pet/comment/dog/comment101",
      "/pet/comment/dog/comment102"
    ]
}
// referenced Comment documents with reference to
// the parent document
{
  "docUri": "/pet/comment/dog/comment101",
  "dogUri": "/pet/dog/dog28261913",
  "name": "Sandy Davis",
  "text": "Fanny is the sweetest dog ever!"
}
```

```
{
  "docUri": "/pet/comment/dog/comment102",
  "dogUri": "/pet/dog/dog28261913",
  "name": "Steve Hoberman",
  "text": "Fanny loved my daughter's brownies."
}
```

Note that a relational model would usually not have an array of *pets*. Joins in relational databases support scalar values, so references are not implemented in both directions. With MarkLogic, only use the references on the side from which you want to access the other objects. Maintaining bidirectional references is more expensive to manage. To summarize referencing, use a scalar to reference a *one* and an array to reference a *many*. Add the references in the main objects from which you will query the data.

Rules and guidelines for embedding and referencing

There are two main rules to follow when deciding between embedding and referencing. Both of these rules adhere to the *MarkLogic Schema Design Principles*:

R1: What is used together, stays together

Adhering to the query-driven design approach, keep data used together in the same document to avoid joins or reads. Joins are costly in terms of CPU and I/O access. Avoiding joins gives much better performance. If each occurrence of the essential query goes from doing three reads and two joins to only one read where the three pieces of information are embedded, you may have just slashed your hardware requirements by a factor of three.

When embedding, keep in mind document size and avoid document bloat by excluding unnecessary information. The reason is that reading this document will take up more space in memory, limiting the number of documents you can keep in memory at a given time.

R2: Favor embedding over referencing

The main reason is that complete objects are usually more straightforward for your application, simpler to archive, and do not require transactions to be updated atomically. In other words, you choose simplicity over complexity by embedding over referencing.

In addition to these rules, there are eleven guidelines. Each guideline has a question for which a yes or no answer determines whether embedding or referencing is appropriate.

To illustrate the guidelines, we will use a simple example of a train schedule for a freight railroad. A freight train transports commodities from an origin to a destination over the rail network. In the abridged Business Term Model (BTM) in Figure 7.4, we have identified the major entities involved in an application that manages train schedules.

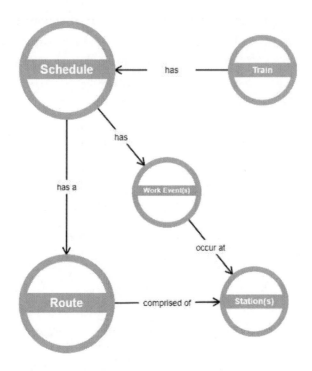

Figure 7.4: Train Schedule business term model.

- A train is required to have a schedule that records the train id, origin, destination, scheduled departure time, and other attributes.

- A train travels a route from origin to destination, which is recorded as a sequence of stations the train will pass through on the rail network. The schedule records each station's planned and actual arrival/departure times. Trains with long routes may consist of hundreds of stations.

- A train will simply pass through some stations while at others the train will stop for work events such as crew change, refueling, inspections, etc.

- As the train travels the route, tracking and other information frequently update the schedule, adjusting the planned and actual arrival/departure times for each station. The larger nodes (circles) for the Route and Schedule entities are used to denote this update frequency in the model.

G1: Simplicity

Would keeping the pieces of information together lead to a simpler data model and code? This is directly related to our rule in favor of embedding and data design focus. In our example, having one object for a train schedule along with the route and work events results in simpler code.

G2: Go Together

Do the pieces of information (the entities) have a has-a, contains, or similar relationship? To determine if pieces of information go together, you examine the relationship between the entities that contain the information. These types of relationships denote a dependency of one piece of information on another. In the BTM model, a schedule *has-a* route and route is *comprised-of* stations. The schedule also *has* work events which *occur-at* a station on the route. Since all these relationships indicate a strong degree of togetherness, let's answer 'yes.'

G3: Query Atomicity

Does the application query the pieces of information together? The train schedule application wants to load the entire schedule with the route and work events, so let's again answer 'yes.'

G4: Update Atomicity

Are the pieces of information updated together? Similar to query atomicity but from a data update perspective. Recall from the BTM, the route information is updated frequently and independently from the main schedule data. Therefore, we answer 'no' to this question.

Let's pause here. We answered 'yes' three times, leading to choosing 'embedding.' But what happened when we answered 'no?' For the first four rules, a 'no' has no impact. In other words, answering 'no' does not favor embedding, but it also does not tell us we should reference.

G5: Archival

Should the pieces of information be archived at the same time? As in our example, this question is only relevant if the system must archive data for regulatory reasons. The essence is that it is easier to archive a single document with all the information in it than a bunch of smaller pieces that would need to be reattached or joined together in the future when looking at the archived information.

For the train schedule application, the answer is 'yes.' After the train has arrived at its destination and the schedule is no longer active, we want the entire schedule archived for analytic and regulatory purposes.

G6: Cardinality

Is there a high cardinality (current or growing) on the many side of the relationship? For very long routes, there could be hundreds of stations and related information (e.g., arrival and departure time at the station).

This guideline does not just favor *referencing* in the affirmative. It favors *embedding* in the negative. This reflects the bias we have toward preferring *embedding.* If the answer is *yes*, we want to avoid embedding large arrays. These large arrays make for large documents, and by experience, we know that usually, the information in large arrays is not entirely needed all the time with the base document. Also, consider the query requirements of the application, as searching individual items (objects) of a large array can pose performance issues.

G7: Data Duplication

Would data duplication be too complicated to manage and undesired? A one-to-many relationship does not generate data duplication, so we have a 'no' to this question.

G8: Document Size

Would the combined size of the pieces of information take too much memory or transfer bandwidth for the application? This is related to the large arrays question, as most big documents contain such large arrays. But here, we want to go further. The document must only be considered 'big' by the consuming application. If it is a mobile application, we are likely more conscious about how much data is transferred. For our example, including schedules with many stations, the total size should be relatively small, even for our mobile applications.

G9: Document Growth

Would the embedded piece grow without bound? This question is also related to the document size. However, it also factors in the impact of often updating the same document by adding new elements in arrays. Keeping the information in different documents will make for smaller write operations. In our example, the documents would have little to no growth over time.

G10: Workload

Are the pieces of information written at different times in a write-heavy workload? A write-heavy workload will benefit from writing to different documents and avoiding the contention of writing to the same documents often. The train schedule example has a write-heavy workload for the route component to update estimated arrival times for each station, which is driven by frequent tracking information events. The answer is 'yes' in favor of referencing.

G11: Individuality

For the children's side of the relationship, can the pieces exist by themselves without a parent? For our example, let's say *no*. While it may be possible to manage routes without a schedule, the application currently manages routes using the schedule. If a route could exist without a schedule, then embedding the route into the schedule would cause an issue when we delete the schedule and the route must continue to exist. Relationships, where both sides may exist alone, are better modeled with separate documents.

Guideline Name	Question	Yes	No
Simplicity	Would keeping the pieces of information together lead to a simpler data model and code?	Embed	
Go Together	Do the pieces of information have a *has-a*, *contains*, or similar relationship?	Embed	
Query Atomicity	Does the application query the pieces of information together?	Embed	
Update Atomicity	Are the pieces of information updated together?	Embed	
Archival	Should the pieces of information be archived at the same time?	Embed	
Cardinality	Is there a high cardinality (current or growing) in a *many* side of the relationship?	Reference	Embed
Data Duplication	Would data duplication be too complicated to manage and undesired?	Reference	Embed
Document Size	Would the combined size of the pieces of information take too much memory or transfer bandwidth for the application?	Reference	Embed
Document Growth	Would the embedded piece grow without bound?	Reference	Embed
Workload	Are the pieces of information written at different times in a write-heavy workload?	Reference	
Individuality	For the children's side of the relationship, can the pieces exist by themselves without a parent?	Reference	

Table 7.1: Embed versus reference guidelines.

Guideline Name	Question	Yes	No
Simplicity	Would keeping the pieces of information together lead to a simpler data model and code?	Embed	
Go Together	Do the pieces of information have a *has-a*, *contains*, or similar relationship?	Embed	
Query Atomicity	Does the application query the pieces of information together?	Embed	
Update Atomicity	Are the pieces of information updated together?	Embed	
Archival	Should the pieces of information be archived at the same time?	Embed	
Cardinality	Is there a high cardinality (current or growing) in a *many* side of the relationship?	Reference	Embed
Data Duplication	Would data duplication be too complicated to manage and undesired?	Reference	Embed
Document Size	Would the combined size of the pieces of information take too much memory or transfer bandwidth for the application?	Reference	Embed
Document Growth	Would the embedded piece grow without bound?	Reference	Embed
Workload	Are the pieces of information written at different times in a write-heavy workload?	Reference	
Individuality	For the children's side of the relationship, can the pieces exist by themselves without a parent?	Reference	

Table 7.2: Train Schedule application answers.

Tallying the results, it is clear we should embed the route and work events with the train schedule. If we had answers for both "embedding" and "referencing," we would consider the priority of each guideline regarding our application requirements.

In the case of ambiguity between "embedding" and "referencing," it would make this relationship a good candidate to apply a schema design pattern, which we will discuss later.

Schema design patterns

Our role with this book is to inform you of all the possibilities, cover the pros and cons, and share use cases. This should inspire readers as they design their schemas. It is a toolbox. Then, it is up to the reader to choose the most appropriate tool for their use cases.

MarkLogic design patterns are reusable solutions for many commonly occurring use cases encountered when designing applications that leverage persistence in MarkLogic.

Note that you don't necessarily need to use the same pattern for reads and for writes. CQRS (Command and Query Responsibility Segregation) is an architecture pattern that prescribes splitting the query operations from the write/update operations. This separation of concerns can bring more flexibility, improved scalability, and enhanced performance. The higher complexity, however, implies a steeper learning curve and higher development costs. However, MarkLogic eases data synchronization by providing full ACID support. MarkLogic guarantees that an insert, update, or delete is durable before acknowledging that it was made, and it guarantees that an insert, update, or delete will be replicated to all the servers in the cluster before a read can take place.

It is not because a pattern exists that you should use it. Using the wrong pattern for a particular use case can be damaging. For example, don't automatically normalize because that's what you're used to doing with relational databases. Involve subject matter experts to ensure that the design satisfies the business needs, not just the developers' convenience. Take into consideration the access patterns. Optimize the user experience. Leverage workflow diagrams, CRUD wireframes, and documented workload analysis. Use an Entity-Relationship Diagram for your PDM to engage in a dialog with all the application stakeholders. Iterate enough to think through the details. Validate schema designs. Realize that the schema will evolve over time as new requirements appear or as reality sheds new light on assumptions.

There are a few ways to think about *Schema Design Patterns* (SDP) considering their categorization, difficulty of usage, and application.

The *Computation* category contains patterns that pre-calculate or assemble data to speed up operations.

The *Grouping* category contains patterns that combine many or parts of documents into a single document.

The *Lifecycle* category contains patterns that have *Operations*. Operations are scripts or procedures performed outside the application at a given time in the system's lifecycle.

The *Polymorphism* category contains patterns designed around the polymorphic characteristic of the document model. If you need a refresher on polymorphism, please refer to the *About the Book* section. This characteristic allows objects with different shapes to live in one collection for various reasons.

The *Relationships* category contains patterns that go beyond simply embedding or referencing to model the relationships between documents. For example, patterns in this category may pivot data or model graphs.

Table 7.3 summarizes our *Schema Design Patterns* grouped by categories.

Category	Patterns
Computation	• Approximation
	• Computed
Grouping	• Bucket
Lifecycle	• Document Versioning
	• Envelope
	• Schema Versioning
Polymorphism	• Polymorphic
Relationships	• Attribute
	• Extended Reference
	• Subset
	• Semantic Graph

Table 7.3: Schema design patterns by category.

We also group patterns based on how easy they are to understand and how frequently we encounter them.

The list of the six basic patterns below is an excellent place to start, as they are the easiest to understand. The following five are quite advanced patterns, meaning they are more difficult to understand or implement. However, they may bring a lot of performance improvements to the application. Finally, for completeness, we have five more patterns that we use less frequently. Nevertheless, they have their place in some designs. Table 7.4 summarizes *Schema Design Patterns* by their difficulty level.

Difficulty	Patterns
Basic	• Approximation • Computed • Extended Reference • Polymorphic • Envelope • Schema Versioning
Advanced	• Attribute • Bucket • Subset
Less common	• Document Versioning • Semantic Graph

Table 7.4: Schema design patterns by difficulty.

Table 7.5 illustrates some attributes of each pattern. One important attribute is the introduction or absence of anomalies. If you recall, anomalies refer to data duplication, staleness, and broken referential integrity.

Finally, we illustrate each pattern with scenarios that use it. Selecting five domains (financial services, e-commerce, Internet of Things, customer service, and a website) and a typical application for each domain, we illustrate a specific requirement that may benefit from applying a given pattern.

Our advisor application for the financial services domain allows different advisors to manage their direct clients. The advisors use the application to get a complete picture of clients and track their interactions. In other words, it is like a Customer Relationship Management system for the advisors.

Pattern	Category	Model Relationship (Yes/No)	Introduce Anomalies (S=some)
Approximation	Computation	N	Y
Attribute	Relationship	Y	N
Bucket	Grouping	Y	N
Computed	Computation	N	Y
Document Versioning	Lifecycle	N	N
Envelope	Lifecycle	N	N
Extended Reference	Relationship	Y	Y
Polymorphic	Polymorphism	Y	N
Schema Versioning	Lifecycle	N	N
Semantic Graph	Relationship	Y	S
Subset	Relationship	Y	Y

Table 7.5: Some attributes of schema design patterns.

The shopping site for the e-commerce domain is similar to Amazon, Walmart, and other sites where we shop.

The SIM cards system for the Internet of Things (IoT) domain is a solution to connect many devices (cars, fridges, etc.) to a single monitoring system. In this case, the devices use the cellular network to communicate with the server using SIM cards.

The single-view application for the customer service domain is an application that provides a complete view of a customer in a complex environment. For example, an insurance company may have acquired many competitors over the years. Merging all the legacy databases into one single MarkLogic database is a very common scenario. The single database allows a customer support representative to see all the information regarding one customer easily and quickly.

And finally, the movies site is a typical website with reference data. The site has many concurrent users. Therefore, we prepare the data to be quickly accessed and displayed in a browser or mobile application.

We will need to be very creative in using every pattern in the context of the Pet Adoption application. Some new requirements may look funny; hopefully, you will think they are. Play with your imagination with the following additional requirements.

- Track, if available, the pet's mother.

- Let people comment on breeds to help other users decide if this is the right breed for them.

- Record the pet room for each pet.

- Allow a pet to have an 𝕏 account. Some are real celebrities with a lot of followers. These pets are too valuable; they are not up for adoption.

- Allow visitors to interact with our pets. We are required to keep a record of the interactions.

- Keep these visitor interactions for the duration of the pet's stay, or in the case of our permanent residents, the pet's life.

- Enable users to purchase pet celebrity swag and merchandise through our online store.

Pattern	Financial Services (Advisor app)	E-commerce (Shopping site)	IoT (SIM cards)	Customer Service (Single View)	Website (Movies site)
Approximation		Web page counters	Counter for connected devices		Web page counters
Attribute	Search for customers' info	Product attributes		Document searchable criteria	Movie revenues per selected countries
Bucket	Transaction per account per month		Measurements for a day	Claims per account per year	Movie revenues per day
Computed	Value of accounts at end of day	Total sales over a period, inventory management	Sums and averages per bucket	Customer representative productivity (number of calls attended per day, duration, etc.)	Revenues from ticket sales
Document Versioning	Audit trail on changes	Changes in the last month	Device upgrades, re-assignments		
Envelope	Application migration, lineage	Application migration, lineage	Application migration, lineage	Application migration, lineage	Application migration, lineage
Extended Reference	Accounts in customer profile	Products in order	Device in measurement	Customer in policy	Actor in movie
Semantic Graph	Identifying possible fraudulent transactions between entities	Multi-categories product hierarchy	Connections between devices	Connections between customers	Recommendations

Pattern	Financial Services (Advisor app)	E-commerce (Shopping site)	IoT (SIM cards)	Customer Service (Single View)	Website (Movies site)
Polymorphic	Grouping different credit products	Grouping different product types	Grouping SIMs from different manufacturers	Grouping policies	Grouping movies and TV shows
Schema Versioning	Application updates	Application updates	Application updates	Application updates	Application updates
Subset	Last N transactions in an account	Product's reviews	Recently reported data for a device	Log of customer's interactions	Movie's reviews

Table 7.6: Schema design patterns, use cases, and scenarios.

The Approximation Pattern

An approximation is a value that is close to the true value, but not an exact match. Approximations are useful when calculating an exact value is not cost effective or is cumbersome to achieve and where a *close enough* value is sufficient.

A benefit of pre-aggregated values (see *The Computed Pattern*) is that we can quickly and efficiently perform additional statistical calculations using those values in the document. What if, however, you needed to perform calculations using aggregate values over many different documents? For example, calculating an average utilizing pre-aggregated values from many sensor documents in an IoT use case. If the accuracy of this calculation does not need to be precise, an approximation could suffice. This is one area where the Approximation Pattern is useful.

Consider the following two sets of questions.

Set 1:
1. What is the current stock price of company X?
2. What is the current exchange rate between USD and Euro?
3. What is the current price of a barrel of oil?
4. How many flights are currently delayed at airport W?

Set 2:
1. What is the current population of earth?
2. How many subscribers does my YouTube channel have at this moment?

3. How many cars have been produced in the US this year?
4. How many users have visited my website?

In both sets of questions, the data is dynamic and subject to frequent updates, rendering the answers inaccurate the moment they are provided. However, for Set 1, precise answers are crucial for driving critical and impactful business decisions. On the other hand, for Set 2, a 'good enough' answer suffices as it will not significantly impact critical business decisions. Additionally, obtaining the exact answer might be challenging or resource-expensive (time, memory, and CPU). In situations where accuracy is not the highest priority, the Approximation Pattern is a suitable approach. If accuracy is of the highest priority, consider using the Compute Pattern.

Description of the Approximation Pattern

The primary aim of the Approximation Pattern is to minimize the write operations, thereby reducing resource usage and facilitating the computation of approximate answers readily available for consumption.

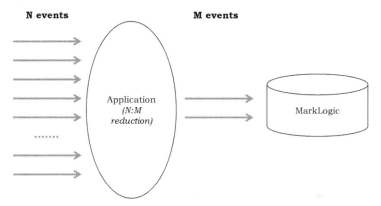

N events   **M events**

Application
(N:M reduction)

MarkLogic

Figure 7.5: Writes to disk.

The Approximation Pattern encompasses the following variants:

- **Windowed aggregation**. This variant involves performing aggregations or analytic functions on data across a window specified by either time or a mathematical approximation function. The aggregation values are written when the time window expires, and the function returns a specific value.

- **Applying Constant Random variable**. In this variant, a constant random variable is calculated, and writes are performed only when the variable value is reached. The consistent randomness helps distribute the computational load evenly, leading to a reduction in resource demands.

- **Applying Geometrical Random variable**. This variant introduces a geometrically distributed random variable. The pattern follows a geometric progression, strategically distributing writes to achieve a balance between precision and resource efficiency in generating approximate answers.

Implementing the Approximation Pattern

Windowed Aggregations

The Windowed Aggregations variant of the Approximation Pattern involves buffering events in an external messaging system like Kafka. The events are collected and aggregated, reducing them to a more condensed set before being written to MarkLogic. If the data arrives as a continuous stream, Kafka Stream Processing can group the events into *windows,* typically defined over a specific time period or size. This approach optimizes the use of resources and allows for more efficient handling of data by consolidating and processing events in a controlled manner before persisting them.

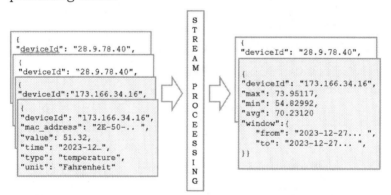

Figure 7.6: Write workload reduction using windowed aggregation.

Constant Random Variable

This approach is suitable when maintaining an estimate, such as the total number of website visitors, is required. As a first step of implementation, define the desired precision or acceptable level of inaccuracy based on a specific use case. Whenever a user visit event is reported, typically from a UI component, generate a random number within the range of 0 to 100. If the generated random number is 0, increment the counter on the server by 100. This approach ensures that writes are performed only when a rare event (random number being 0) occurs, reducing the frequency of updates. The assumed affordable inaccuracy is reflected in the probability distribution, with a counter increment occurring only 1/100 times. This helps strike a balance between precision and resource efficiency, particularly when minor inaccuracies are tolerable for estimation.

Geometrical Random Writes

We apply this approach in situations similar to the Constant Random Variable. The difference is that a geometrical distribution is used instead of a constant random variable value when determining when to write. For the same example of the scenario, we want the estimate of the daily clicks on a website. Let us choose a geometrical distribution with a probability of success(p) of 0.05 (5%). The random number is generated using this formula for different values of k:

$$P(X = 1) = (1 - 0.05)^0 \times 0.05 = 0.05$$
$$P(X = 2) = (1 - 0.05)^1 \times 0.05 = 0.0475$$
$$P(X = 3) = (1 - 0.05)^2 \times 0.05 = 0.0451$$

...

The counter is incremented on the server by k based on the generated random number. In this way, updates occur less frequently, and the system adapts to the probability distribution, allowing for resource-efficient estimation of daily clicks while introducing controlled randomness.

Figure 7.7 contains a simple algorithm. There are a lot of alternate algorithms in the literature, which can be more complex depending on the specific use case.

Reducing the number of writes also helps the system with concurrency. If the counter resides in one document per product, this document will undergo massive concurrent locks and potential write conflicts.

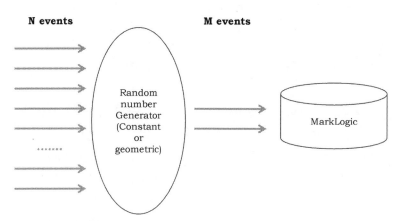

Figure 7.7: Illustration of reducing database writes.

Applying the Approximation Pattern to our case study

There are a few other situations where the *Approximation Pattern* would apply. Usually, the cases fall into one of the following categories.

- Data is difficult to calculate correctly.
- Data is expensive to calculate.
- Imprecise numbers are acceptable.

We can use the Approximation Pattern to track the number of webpage views on our site. Implementing the pattern is straightforward from a data modeling perspective: simply include a counter in the document. In this instance, we will add a counter named *webPageViews* to the pet document. A sample document structure is as follows

```
// a Pet document with a counter for the web page
// views.
{
    "pet": {
        "petId": "bird102345",
        "petName": "Lady G",
        ...
        "webPageViews": 187244
    }
}
```

The schema for this document looks like this:

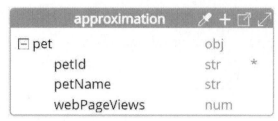

Figure 7.8: Approximation schema example.

In the final step, the application code is modified to update the counters using one of the discussed variants.

Benefits of the Approximation Pattern

The Approximation Pattern offers several benefits, with the primary advantage being the optimal utilization of resources without significant business disadvantages. Beyond resource efficiency, there are additional advantages associated with this pattern:

- **Concurrency improvement**. By reducing the number of writes, the pattern alleviates concurrency issues within the system. In scenarios like the counter example, where multiple user-visit events may trigger updates to the same document, minimizing writes helps mitigate concurrent locks and write conflicts. This is particularly important for maintaining system performance and responsiveness.

- **Lock handling optimization**. In the counter example, where the counter resides in a single document, reporting every user-visit event could lead to extensive concurrent locks and potential write conflicts. The Approximation Pattern helps optimize lock handling, as the reduced frequency of writes diminishes the likelihood of conflicts. Although MarkLogic handles locks automatically with retries, minimizing unnecessary lock contention is a wise usage of server resources.

- **Resource-efficient approximation**. The pattern allows for the acceptance of approximation in scenarios where precise values are not critical. This acceptance of a certain level of inaccuracy contributes to resource efficiency, making it a pragmatic choice when exact precision is not a strict requirement for a given use case.

In summary, the Approximation Pattern not only conserves resources but also addresses issues related to concurrency and lock handling, and provides a balanced approach to achieving efficient and acceptable results for certain types of data and applications.

Trade-offs with the Approximation Pattern

The Approximation Pattern's main trade-off lies in intentionally introducing inaccuracy for the sake of resource efficiency. While it offers benefits in terms of optimized resource usage, the compromise is accuracy. The system's suitability depends on well-defined acceptable limits of inaccuracy, making it appropriate for applications where minor errors are tolerable. However, precision-critical contexts or scenarios with dynamic conditions may find this pattern less suitable. Managing user expectations and carefully evaluating specific requirements are crucial for making informed decisions when considering the Approximation Pattern.

Summary of the Approximation Pattern

The Approximation Pattern is a straightforward approach designed to minimize resource usage for data that can tolerate imperfections. Implementation of this pattern occurs directly within the application.

Problem	• High resource usage from write operations for keeping a perfect state where it is not required
Solution	• Reduce the frequency of write operations • Increase the payload done by the write operations
Use cases	• Web page counters • Other high-value counters • Statistics • IoT data analysis

Benefits	• Reduces the number of write operations
	• Reduces write operation contention on documents
	• Statistically valid numbers
Trade-offs	• Potentially creates imperfect numbers
	• Must be implemented in the application.

Table 7.7: The Approximation Pattern.

The Attribute Pattern

Polymorphism is one of the most powerful attributes of the document model. It allows putting objects with different characteristics into one schema/document. But what if you can't predict the difference between objects and want to query these fields? In a traditional relational database, one would transpose or pivot a list of flexible attributes in a table and join them with the object ID. Each row has a foreign key to the main table, an attribute name, and its value. This modeling technique is known as *entity-attribute-value* and by other names such as *object-attribute-value* and *vertical schema*. Since this is a 1-M relationship, we can do the same in MarkLogic by using arrays of objects in conjunction with appropriate indexes.

Description of the Attribute Pattern

The core idea of the Attribute Pattern is to group many similar properties into an array of subobjects. The subobjects will minimally consist of two name-value pairs. Additional name-value pair properties can be added to the subobject as required. We can use standardized abstract (non-deterministic) property names to make indexing easier.

This pattern can benefit catalog applications where many fields describe a product. This pattern is also advantageous for conducting searches across these many fields.

Let's start by reviewing the *Attribute Pattern.* Then, using our example application use case, include an example utilizing the Wildcard Indexes functionality.

The *Attribute Pattern* has these variants:

Using a name-value pair.
Using a name-value pair and additional qualifiers.

In a traditional relational database, we often represent an undefined list of columns for a given row as an attribute table. The attribute table is a pivot of the unpredictable columns. A one-to-many relationship exists between the original row and the attribute table.

When using this pattern, we use a similar layout for MarkLogic.

- The column for the name of an attribute becomes property name "k": "*property name*"

- The column for the value of the attribute becomes "v": "*property value*".

The resulting document is more difficult to read and feels different than a usual JSON document.

We then create an index for each property in the subobject. Since MarkLogic range indexes cover only one property, a minimum of two indexes is required.

Implementing the Attribute Pattern

Take these steps to implement the *Attribute Pattern*:

- Identify the properties to group together.

- Create an array that will contain these targeted properties.

- For each targeted property, create a subobject in the array.

- For each subobject, the target property's name becomes the value of k, while the value becomes the value of v.

- For additional qualifiers (q1, q2, ...), an additional property should tie the values. The additional property should be consistent across the targeted properties, especially the data type.

- Create the appropriate index for each property k, v, q1, q2, ...

For example, the fields representing the prices in the following document look initially like this.

```
{
  "productID": "12345",
  "productName": "The Little Prince",
  . . .
  "priceUSA": 9. 99
  "priceFrance": 15. 00
}
```

Figure 7.9 shows the schema for the above document.

Figure 7.9: Attribute pattern schema example 1.

We have this after applying the Attribute Pattern:

```
{
  "product": {
      "id": "12345",
      "name": "The Little Prince",
      "prices": [
          {
              "k": "priceUSA",
              "v": 9.99,
              "q": "USD"
          },
          {
            "k": "priceFrance",
            "v": 15.00,
            "q": "Euros"
          }
      ]
  }
}
```

Figure 7.10 shows the schema for the above document.

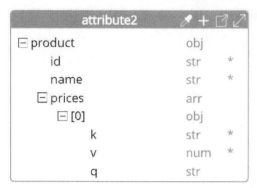

Figure 7.10: Attribute pattern schema example 2.

Applying the Attribute Pattern to our case study

We use the Attribute Pattern to model some fields we want to use to search for pets. We do not want to create an index for each newly added search criterion. The search page will have a drop-down menu for each search criterion. The document may look like:

```
// a Pet document with attributes
{
  "petId": "bird102345",
  "petName": "Lady G",
  "details": [
    "character": "independent",
    "color": "green",
    "height": 0.2,      // 0.2 m or 20 cm
    "origin": "Venezuela",
    "voice": "marvelous",
    "weight": 0.3     // 0.3 kg or 300 g
  ]
}
```

Let's use the Attribute Pattern with a qualifier for the relationships between the keys and values. Pivoting the attributes gives us the following document.

```
// a Pet document with attributes
{
  "pet": {
    "id": "bird102345",
    "petName": "Lady G",
    "details": [
      { "k": "character", "v": "independent" },
      { "k": "color", "v": "green", "q": "dark" },
      { "k": "height", "v": "20", "q": "cm" },
      { "k": "origin", "v": "Venezuela" },
      { "k": "voice", "v": "marvelous" },
      { "k": "weight", "v": "300", "q": "g" }
    ]
  }
}
```

Figure 7.11 shows the schema for the above document.

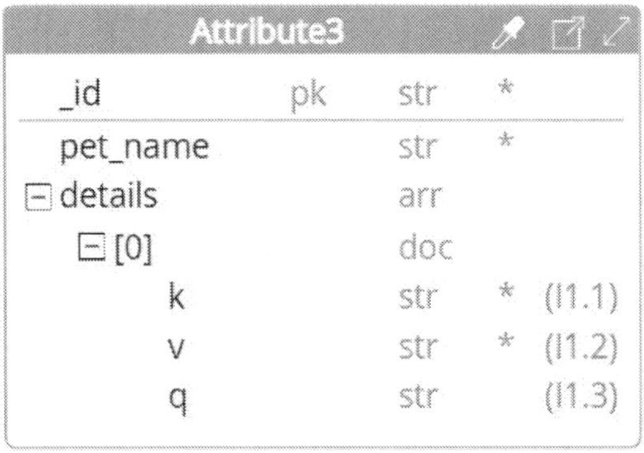

Figure 7.11: Attribute pattern schema example 3.

Then, we create the following indexes.

```
const admin = require('/MarkLogic/admin. xqy');
const config = admin.getConfiguration();
const dbID = xdmp.database("petDB");
const collation =
 http://marklogic. com/collation/codepoint;
// Enable Word and Value positions for indexes on the
database
let updtConfig =
admin.databaseSetElementWordPositions(config,
xdmp.database("petDB"), fn.true());
let updtConfig =
admin.databaseSetElementValuePositions(config,
xdmp.database("petDB"), fn.true());
// Create path range index on "k"
let updtConfig = admin.databaseAddRangePathIndex (
     config,
     dbID,
     admin.databaseRangePathIndex(
       "string",
       "/petId/details/k",
       collation,
       fn.false(),
       "ignore"
     )
   );
// Create path range index on "v"
let updtConfig = admin.databaseAddRangePathIndex(
     config,
     dbID,
     admin.databaseRangePathIndex(
       "string",
       "/petId/details/v",
       collation,
       fn.false(),
       "ignore"
     )
   );
```

```
// Create path range index on "q"
let updtConfig = admin.databaseAddRangePathIndex(
      config,
      dbID,
      admin.databaseRangePathIndex (
        "string",
        "/petId/details/q",
        collation,
        fn.false(),
        "ignore"
      )
    );
// Save updated database configuration.
admin.saveConfiguration(updtConfig);
This query would find a pet that is dark green:
var query =
cts.jsonPropertyScopeQuery("/petId/details",
 cts.andQuery(
   [cts.jsonPropertyValueQuery("k","color"),
    cts.jsonPropertyValueQuery("v","green"),
    cts.jsonPropertyValueQuery("q","dark"),
   ]
  )
 );
cts.search(query,"unfiltered");
```

You will want to design your groups to limit the number of distinct qualifier properties you want to search to keep the number of indexes manageable.

Benefits of the Attribute Pattern

The attribute pattern can potentially reduce the number of indexes in the database when you have many properties you need to search. Additionally, it provides the flexibility of adding new characteristics or details to an entity that are not thought of now but appear later without schema and modeling changes.

Instead of keeping an eye on new properties in the document to create additional indexes, the Attribute Pattern allows these new attributes to be added automatically as part of the limited number of indexes covering the properties in the group.

Trade-offs with the Attribute Pattern

The resulting representation of a document is less readable because the structure departs from the name-value representation used for the other parts of the document.

Furthermore, we must enable the *element word positions* and *element value positions* database properties to add property position details to the indexes. By default, these are disabled to save space and improve ingestion throughput. Otherwise, querying on two properties without position information will return any document with a subobject matching the first condition and a second subobject matching the second condition.

Summary of the Attribute Pattern

The *Attribute Pattern* allows indexing a set of properties at once. This ability is handy when there are unpredictable property names. It removes the difficulty in creating indexes on these unpredictable names.

Problem	• Many unpredictable keys in documents need to be indexed
Solution	• Rearrange the properties as name-value pairs
Use cases	• Product characteristics. • Set of properties with the same value type
Benefits	• Lowers the number of indexes • Allows considering new key names automatically by an index
Trade-offs	• The pattern's k-v-q notation differs and is less readable than the other properties in the document • Position indexes must be enabled in the database

Table 7.8: The Attribute Pattern

The Bucket Pattern

When data arrives as a stream over time (e.g., events or time-series data), we may be inclined to store each measurement in its own document as if we were using a relational database. This results in a potentially huge number of documents for a specific logical document. In the train schedule example, if we stored each train tracking event in the database for each train id, we could end up with thousands of documents for one train schedule. To enable fast query access, we could do one of the following.

- Create a range index on the event timestamp and use collection names that include train id and event type to narrow down the query scope
- Construct document URI containing train id, event type, and timestamp.

While either of the above enables fast queries, you could still return thousands of documents, which may not work well for your application. Another approach would be to *bucket* the data, by time, into documents that hold the events from a particular time span. This approach allows you to *right size* the documents for your application and reduce the number of documents returned. We can also programmatically add additional information to each of these buckets. Other benefits of *bucketing* include:

- Savings on index size
- Potential query simplification

- Ability to use pre-aggregated data in documents.

Description of the Bucket Pattern

The Bucket Pattern is an intermediate or middle ground solution between embedding and referencing. It's also useful for grouping many small related documents in a more manageable size. We often see the Bucket Pattern with Internet of Things (IoT) data, time series data, and any relationship with high cardinality. For example, one may want to group the measurements of a device or the revenues over a month for a given theater.

By grouping individual pieces of information into buckets, we have documents with a predictable size optimized for the system. One common quandary when applying this pattern is the amount of grouping we need. As said above, the resulting size of the document is one criterion.

Another critical question is how the application and the users will query the data later. For example, let's say an aggregation query is the most critical operation in terms of latency. To illustrate this, let's say the bucket for a document is a month of data. The most critical query needs to calculate daily averages from the values in the bucket to report these in the UI. Then this query tells us that a daily grouping may be more optimal.

When the workload has tight requirements for write and read operations, the solution may use a document with a bucket to capture the data at the proper grouping and another document to keep the data in a single document to speed up the read operations. The Computed Pattern is often used to precompute the operations on a bucket. In the example case above, the daily average could have been pre-calculated and stored in a bucket in another document.

Implementing the Bucket Pattern

To implement the Bucket Pattern, take the following steps:

- Identify the granularity of the bucket
- Create an array to group the measurement or data
- Identify a field at the document's root that identifies the bucket, like a date for time series data or a bucket number for entities bucketed by size.

Applying the Bucket Pattern to our case study

On average, our pets get two to three interactions a week. Creating a document for each interaction seems excessive. On the other hand, putting all the interactions in the pet document will make archiving the documents a little more complicated than we want, so we will use the *Bucket Pattern* to model the interactions.

The first question relates to the granularity of the bucket. A week leads to very few observations per bucket, while a year may give too many and make the archiving operation a little more complicated than needed. Hence, we settle for a granularity of month.

Adding the measurements under the field `interactions` and identifying the bucket by the month in `month`, the documents in the interactions collection look like this:

```
// an Interaction document with a bucket of
// monthly interactions
{
  "mthlyPetInteractions": {
    "petId": "bird102345",
    "month": "2023-02-01T00:00:00Z",
    "Interactions": [
        {
        "tmstmp": "2023-02-14T22:14:00Z",
        "userid": 34717
        },
        {
        "tmstmp": "2023-02-15T20:00:00Z",
        "userid": 31043
        },
        . . .
    ]
  }
}
```

Figure 7.12 shows the schema for the above document, in the ERD.

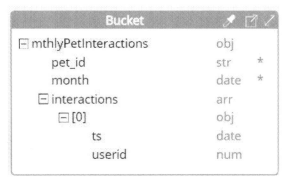

Figure 7.12: Bucket pattern schema example.

Figure 7.13 shows the schema tree view.

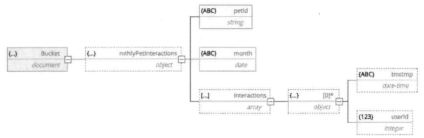

Figure 7.13: Bucket pattern schema tree view.

Benefits of the Bucket Pattern

If the *Bucket Pattern* groups what may have been separate documents, it reduces the number of read operations. On the other hand, if all data points were in one document, that single read may bring more information than needed in memory. The pattern may be a good compromise between the number of read operations and the amount of data read in memory.

The data is organized per unit of time, which makes it more manageable. One can compute summaries for the unit of time and store these computations in the document. For example, a monthly sum of the data stored in the document will make further aggregations faster; summing data for a year is a faster operation on the twelve partial sums than adding potentially thousands of documents every time.

It is easier to archive or delete a set of documents as long as they are a multiple of the grouping unit. For example, archiving three months of data when the grouping is by month is easy. However, archiving one week for documents containing one month of data is a little more complicated.

One possible situation that can arise when using the Bucket Pattern is that there may be large numbers of small groups of data. In the above example, each interaction is a small data element, thus the bucket may contain several hundred entries while staying within an acceptable document size. The consuming application may need to paginate the bucketed data to legibly display the interactions on a user interface. MarkLogic's built-in search APIs (/v1/search) provide pagination over documents but not pagination within the content of documents. However, MarkLogic low-level cts (*core text search*) functions provide this capability. The server module below paginates over interactions with the supplied start and pageLength.

```
XQuery
declare variable $start as xs:long external;
declare variable $pageLength as xs:long external;
let $interactions := cts:search(collection(),
    cts:json-property-value-
query("petId","bird102345"))/
mthlyPetInteractions/Interactions
return $interactions[$start to ($start + $pageLength
- 1)]
Javascript
var start = 1;
var pageLength = 2;
var xpath = "/mthlyPetInteractions/Interactions [" +
start + " to " + pageLength + "]";
fn.head(cts.search(
    cts.jsonPropertyValueQuery("petId",
        "bird102345"))).xpath(xpath)
```

```
Optic Javascript
const op = require("/MarkLogic/optic")
var limit = 5;
var offset = 0;
var query =
cts.andQuery([cts.jsonPropertyValueQuery("petId","bir
d102345")])
op.fromSearchDocs(query)
.bind([
  op.as("col1", op.xpath('doc',
'/mthlyPetInteractions/Interactions'))
 ])
.unnestInner('col1','interaction', 'i')
.select(['i', 'interaction'])
.offset(offset)
.limit(limit)
.result()
```

The above code searches documents with petId = 'bird102345' and returns only a subset of interactions controlled by supplied limits on start and offset. The module can be deployed as a MarkLogic REST extension or a MarkLogic server module to be called as a server evaluation. The optic implementation can also be supplied to /rows built-in REST endpoint.

Additional benefits of *bucketing* include:

- Savings on index size
- Potential query simplification
- Ability to use pre-aggregated data in documents.

Trade-offs with the Bucket Pattern

Queries that operate on sections of a bucket are more challenging to write. Queries that need to unwind the elements of the array first before going further may suffer from performance versus simply adding values in documents.

BI tools typically opt for the relational format as their primary data structure. Even when supporting XML and JSON document formats, such documents need to go through several operations before they are ready for analytic operations for dashboards. Challenges arise when handling JSON arrays and XML repeating elements, as unwinding/unnesting them into a relational format poses unique difficulties. MarkLogic provides the Template Driven Extraction (TDE) feature to tackle this issue. TDE enables you to define a relational lens over your document data so that you can query your data using standard SQL. If necessary, the TDEs unwind the arrays to separate table rows and generate linking keys to the parent tables.

The below TDE generates a view Pet.interactions for the example above.

```
var tde = require("/MarkLogic/tde.xqy");

var interactionsView = xdmp.toJSON(
 {
  "template":{
   "context":"/mthlyPetInteractions/Interactions",
   "rows":[
    {
     "schemaName":"Pet",
     "viewName":"interactions",
     "columns":[
      {
       "name":"petId",
```

```
      "scalarType":"string",
    "val":"../../../mthlyPetInteractions/petId"
      },
      {
       "name":"userid",
       "scalarType":"string",
       "val":"userid"
      },
      {
       "name":"tmstmp",
       "scalarType":"dateTime",
       "val":"tmstmp"
      }
    ]
   }
  ]
 }
 }
 );
tde.templateInsert("Interactions.tdex",
interactionsView);
```

Once the TDE is installed, a SQL query *select * from Pets.interactions desc* will produce the following result.

Pet.interactions.petId	Pet.interactions.userid	Pet.interactions.ts
bird102345	34717	2023-02-14T22:14:00Z
bird102345	31043	2023-02-15T20:00:00Z

One thing to note here is that when the array is flattened, the order of the rows should not be assumed in the same order as in the document. Appropriate sorting on the column should be done in case the output is required in an order.

Summary of the Bucket Pattern

The *Bucket Pattern* is an alternative to fully embedding or referencing relationships. It works best with one-to-many relationships and streaming data. It is a pattern that requires a good understanding of the workload.

Problem	• Avoiding too many documents • Avoiding documents that are too big • A one-to-many relationship that can't be embedded
Solution	• Define the optimal grouping of information • Create an array to store the optimal amount per document
Use cases	• Streaming data • Internet of Things • Time series data • Data Warehouse • One-to-many relationships with high cardinality
Benefits	• Provides a good balance between the number of read accesses and the size of the data returned • Makes the data more manageable • Easy to prune data • Helps implement paging results • Reduces index sizes • Simplify data access by leveraging pre-aggregated data • Potential query simplification

Trade-offs	• Can lead to poor query results if not designed correctly
	• Less friendly to BI tools

Table 7.9: The Bucket Pattern.

The Computed Pattern

The significance of stored data is realized by applying mathematical or statistical methods, generating more meaningful insights from the data. While the bucket pattern largely solves managing the volume of time-series data and other data involving relationships with high cardinality, it does not address the efficient computation of aggregate measures such as counters, rollups, sums, and averages that users of the data typically need. Examples of these types of computations include determining total sales for each region over the last three months or the average flow rate through a pipe over a period of time.

Description of the Computed Pattern

We use the Computed Pattern when we have data that needs to be computed repeatedly in an application. Computing these values each time they are requested can strain or even exhaust resources (CPU, disk, and memory), especially given the current volumes of data in modern contexts. Notably, business intelligence (BI) tools excel in providing rapid answers when working with large datasets due to their ability to pre-calculate responses to common queries. Despite their effectiveness, BI tools often involve batch data loading and lack real-time data access.

The Computed Pattern emerges as a solution when repetitive computations on stored data are necessary, especially in scenarios with a higher frequency of reads than writes. At its core, the Computed Pattern emphasizes pre-computing values before they are required. This pattern finds applicability in situations where there is a significant disparity between reads and writes, real-time generation of computed values is mandated (e. g., over a REST API), or the computation, if not pre-computed, proves resource-intensive (e.g., significant look-back periods or extensive datasets).

After deciding to use the Computed Pattern, determine the optimal point for executing the computation. This pattern is applicable when computations are carried out before their actual need. In MarkLogic, the computations can occur either during ingestion or as part of a batch process. In both scenarios, using aggregate functions will be necessary to apply mathematical and statistical methods.

Aggregate functions operate on values within one or more MarkLogic range indexes, producing a concise set of results. These functions leverage in-database MapReduce[18] for parallel execution across hosts and forests, ensuring proximity to the data.

MarkLogic Server provides built-in aggregate functions for common mathematical and statistical operations. Users can also implement custom aggregate functions using the Aggregate User-Defined Function (UDF) interface. As of MarkLogic version 11, the following aggregate functions are accessible through XQuery, JavaScript, REST, and Java APIs. Table 7.10 is not

---

[18] https://en.wikipedia.org/wiki/MapReduce.

complete and you should always refer to the MarkLogic
Server documentation for the complete list.

XQuery	JavaScript
cts:avg-aggregate	cts.avgAggregate
cts:avg-aggregate .	cts.correlation
cts:correlation	cts.correlation
cts:count-aggregate	cts.countAggregate
cts:covariance	cts.covariance
cts:covariance-p	cts.covarianceP
cts:max	cts.max
cts:median	cts.median
cts:min	cts.min
cts:stddev	cts.stddev
cts:stddev-p	cts.stddevP
cts:sum-aggregate	cts.sumAggregate
cts:variance	cts.variance
cts:variance-p	cts.varianceP

Optic APIs	
XQuery	Javascript
op:array-aggregate	op.arrayAggregate
op:sequence-aggregate	op.sequenceAggregate
op:avg	op.avg
op:count	op.count
op:group-concat	op.groupConcat
op:max	op.Max
op:min	op.min
op:sample	op.sample
op:sum	op.sum
op:group-to-arrays	op.groupToArrays
op:group-by-union	op.groupByUnion
op:cube	op.cube
op:rollup	op.rollup
op:uda*	op.uda*

Table 7.10: Aggregate functions.

If you need an aggregation function other than the ones provided, op:uda allows you to call a User-Defined Function. Since MarkLogic has a built-in SQL engine, we can use all the aggregation mechanisms available in standard ANSI SQL in MarkLogic.

Implementing the Computed Pattern

We can implement the computed pattern in MarkLogic using the following variants.

Variant 1 – Using URIs, collections, and transformations

In MarkLogic, a single document has the flexibility to be linked with multiple collections. The strategic association of documents with meaningful collections presents a straightforward method for pre-aggregating data. Consider a scenario where a system is onboarding devices into an IoT infrastructure. The asset is represented in Figure 7.14.

asset			
ipAddressV4	pk	str	*
manufacturer		str	*
installedDate		date	*
active		bool	
joinDt		date	
latitude		num	
longitude		num	

Figure 7.14: Onboarding devices into an IoT infrastructure.

For instance, when a device is onboarded (joinDt) on November 13th, 2022, the document can be linked to collections such as *Asset, 2022*, and *2022-Q4*. When the need arises to count the number of devices onboarded in 2022-Q4, we can use the following MarkLogic javascript functions:

```
fn.count(fn.collection("2022-Q4"))
```

Here, the implementation will appear not pre-computed because we do the counting when needed. That is only partially true. By assigning the document to the correct collections, computations are indirectly done. In the above example, by assigning all assets onboarded in quarter 4 of 2022 to collection *2022-Q4*, the heavy lifting of counting the number of assets onboarded is already done. The on-demand counting done through the sample code will be very fast in MarkLogic as it is an in-memory operation on the collection lexicon. If it is known upfront that grouping by state or manufacturer is required, we can assign the document to such collections. Even if not all collections are explicitly assigned, the approach remains beneficial due to a significant reduction in the number of documents to inspect for state or manufacturer.

There is no need to predetermine the collection information before data ingestion. If the document contains the necessary information to determine the collections to which it should be assigned, we can achieve this association through transformations during the ingestion process. In Datahub implementations, interceptors offer a mechanism to dynamically assign collections to documents based on their content.

Variant 2 – Batch computation

In the context of implementing scheduled computation tasks, the following steps outline the process:

- **Identify frequent computations**. Recognize and prioritize the frequent computations that are candidates for scheduled aggregation.

- **Determine whether the computations are stored within the document or as RDF triples**. When storing the computation within a document, you can store it in the same or a separate document. For example, it is better to store the quarterly sales count of a product in the master product document than in a separate document that holds various aggregates of that product.

Utilizing the MarkLogic RDF triple-store capability, you can store the calculation as a triple:

`<ProductID>` → `QuantitySoldInQ32023` → `300`

The choice depends on factors such as data organization and retrieval efficiency.

product_details			
productId	pk	str	*
category		str	
productName		str	
⊟ salesCount		arr	
[0] 2023_q4_sales		int	
[1] 2023_q3_sales		int	
[2] 2023_q2_sales		int	
[3] 2023_q1_sales		int	

Figure 7.15: Computed values within the document.

product_computed			
productId	pk	str	*
⊟ salesCount		arr	
[0] 2023_q4_sales		int	
[1] 2023_q3_sales		int	
[2] 2023_q2_sales		int	
[3] 2023_q1_sales		int	

Figure 7.16: Computed values in a separate document.

Figure 7.17: Computed values as a triple.

Decide on the preferred frequency for executing computations, which may vary from regular intervals to specific events, prompting the necessity for aggregation. In the provided instance, an optimal computation time could be the last day of quarter 3. If the business requires intermediate sales counts, performing the aggregation at the end of each month might be suitable. The chosen frequency naturally hinges on the specific demands of the business.

Schedule a script execution either within MarkLogic using Scheduled Tasks or externally orchestrated through a separate script. The script can be implemented in XQuery or Javascript using the APIs listed above.

For the MarkLogic Server, leverage the 'Scheduled Tasks' feature to automate the execution of scripts at defined intervals. For external orchestration, utilize external tools or schedulers to trigger the execution of the aggregation script.

The variant 2 implementation prioritizes the incremental construction of aggregated results, thereby avoiding resource-intensive computations at the time of querying for the computed values. This approach aims to enhance efficiency by pre-calculating and updating results over time, ensuring that the system can provide prompt responses to user queries without incurring heavy computational loads. We can combine the implementation with the approach of strategically assigning collections to further optimize the efficiency of scheduled tasks.

Applying the Computed Pattern to our case study

In our Pet Adoption project, we will apply the Computed Pattern to calculate the interaction summary of the last three completed months. Since interactions are an array within the pet document, the first variant using collections and URIs does not apply. It would apply if interactions were separate documents in such a way that we assign each interaction document to collections calculated using the interaction date.

The second variation does apply, and we will add the interaction summary to the pets document in the attribute `interactions_last_3_months`. The code to compute is assumed to be scheduled at the beginning of the 4th month.

```
/* a Pet document with a sum of interactions for the
last three completed months
```

```
*/
{
  "petId": "bird102345",
  "petName": "Lady G",
    . . .
  // Computed value from the interaction collection
  "interactions_last_3_months": 87
}
```

The schema of the above document is shown in Figure 7.18.

Figure 7.18: Computed pattern schema example.

The JavaScript code using Optic APIs for generating the computation is as follows:

```
/*Code for generating the total interactions for all
pets for the period
2023 Jan, Feb, and March */

const op = require("/MarkLogic/optic")
var query = cts.andQuery([
        cts.collectionQuery("pets")
        ])
 op.fromSearchDocs(query)
 .bind([op.as("coll",
        op.xpath('doc',
            '/interactions/ts'
            ))
    ])
 .unnestInner('coll', 'tmstmp')
```

```
.select([op.as('id',
        op.xs.string(op.xpath('doc',
                    '/petId'))
        ),
    op.as('interactionTime',
        op.xs.dateTime(op.col('tmstmp'))
    )
    ])
.where(op.lt(op.col('interactionTime'),
    '2023-04-01T00:00:01Z')
    )
.where(op.ge(op.col('interactionTime'),
    '2023-01-01T00:00:01Z')
    )
.groupBy(op.col('id'),
op.count("interactions_last_3_months",
        "interactionTime")
    )
.result()
```

If XQuery is the preferred language, the same can be implemented in XQuery. Using Template Driven Extraction (TDE), we can build a relational view and use SQL queries like this:

```
SELECT PET_ID, COUNT(*)
FROM INTERACTIONS
WHERE INTERACTION_TIME BETWEEN <T1> AND <T2>
GROUP BY PET_ID;
```

The implementation is decided based on what best works with your data structure and the preferred programming language.

Benefits of the Computed Pattern

The primary objective of the Computed Pattern is to enhance the speed of read operations. By pre-calculating data ahead of time, read operations become simpler and more efficient. When read operations outnumber writes, computations may be repeatedly performed on the same data, yielding identical results. We can mitigate this redundancy by incorporating the computation into the write operation. This approach reduces the number of computations, resulting in a more efficient utilization of CPU resources.

Trade-offs with the Computed Pattern

There's a risk of read operations fetching outdated data when the read operation is performed before the computation. To mitigate, a good understanding of the business is required to determine how frequently to perform the pre-computes. Another option is to read pre-computed values for some portion of data and perform the computation when needed for the remaining portion that has not yet been computed. For example, suppose the pre-computation is done for the previous quarter (say Q1) at the beginning of the subsequent quarter (say Q2). When the read operation is done at any time in Q2, Q1 data can be read from pre-computed values, but values for the running Quarter 2 are done when needed. The final result is the combination of both values. Generating Q2 values will be comparatively faster because only Q2 data needs to be inspected and computed.

Also, computations may result in data duplication since the calculated values are essentially snapshots of other data at a particular point in time. Consider this factor when evaluating the trade-offs associated with the Computed Pattern.

Summary of the Computed Pattern

The Computed Pattern involves pre-computing data before read operations to mitigate extended retrieval times.

Problem	• Expensive computation or manipulation of data
	• Frequent execution of the same computation on identical data produces identical results
Solution	• Execute the operation and store the result in the appropriate document either at write time or through a scheduler
Use cases	• Internet of Things
	• Event sourcing
Benefits	• Faster read operations
	• Saving CPU and disk access resources
Trade-offs	• Potentially introduces staleness of data
	• Potentially creates duplicated information

Table 7.11: The Computed Pattern.

The Document Versioning Pattern

Tracking the changes and exploring the historical states of a resource, entity, or document is a common requirement. This need is evident in Source Control Systems such as git, CVS, and ClearCase, which maintain a comprehensive file history. Content Management Systems (CMS) also prioritize keeping track of revisions. Does this concept extend to databases?

Databases like MarkLogic can process tons of queries and make frequent updates on the data. However, they usually can only represent the last state of the data. So what if an application necessitates accessing past states of the document? This is where the Document Versioning Pattern becomes valuable.

Description of the Document Versioning Pattern

The Document Versioning Pattern is used to track changes in a document and ensure the availability and usability of the version history of documents.

Implementing the Document Versioning Pattern

There are two basic ways to apply the Document Versioning Pattern:

1. Storing complete document versions
   a. Embed version details in the document or metadata
   b. Store version information in the directory (URI) of the document
   c. Manage versions within collections

      d. Triggers

      e. Utilizing Temporal documents

      f. Leveraging Document Library Services (DLS).

2. Preserving only the differences between versions.

The first variant is more straightforward if we want to look at the full documents, as the second variant needs to reconstruct versions based on differences. The simplicity of the first variant comes at the cost of using more storage for all revisions.

The second variant is more appropriate when many changes happen to documents, and the focus is on who made which change and when it occurred.

Variant 1 – Storing complete document versions

Variant 1 has several implementation methods. Methods 1a, 1b, 1c, and 1d necessitate implementation through client-side and/or server-side code. On the other hand, methods 1e and 1f are inherent features in MarkLogic that automate the version management process. The detailed procedures for implementation-based methods are elaborated in the following sections. High-level explanations are provided for the variants involving temporal documents and Document Library Services (DLS). For more in-depth insights, refer to the product documentation for relevant APIs and examples.

The schema for variant 1 introduces these two properties to the document:

- version number
- update datetime.

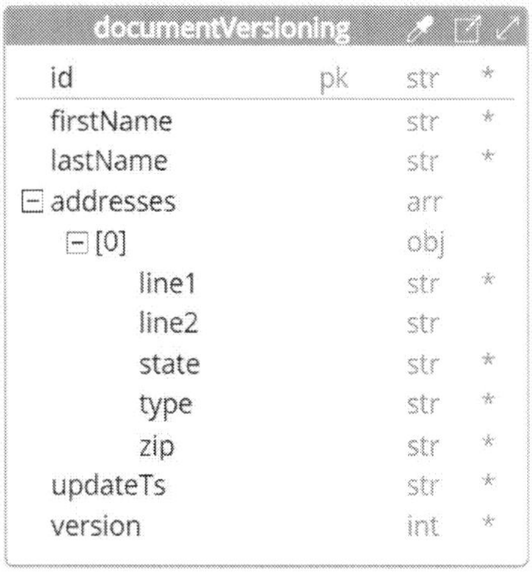

Figure 7.19: Variant 1.

Managing document versions in document, URI, collection, or metadata

This section discusses implementation methods 1a, 1b, and 1c.

Let's first discuss what metadata is in MarkLogic. In addition to storing a document, MarkLogic stores metadata about a document in what is called a properties document. The properties document can be thought of as a *side document* and is only created if properties are created. The properties document shares the same URI with the data document. The metadata is queryable using specific APIs. From here forward, we will refer to the properties document as simply metadata or the metadata document.

The following examples show two versions of a document, including metadata, URI, and collections.

```
URI:/users/11/10002.json
Metadata: version = 11
Collections: v11, users
{
"User": {
"id": "10002",
"firstName": "Amargo",
"lastName": "Leyburn",
"addresses": [
     {"address": {
   "line1": "79859 Fairview Roa",
   "city": "Brooklyn",
   "state": "NY",
   "type": "Communication",
   "zip": "11225"
}
}],
"updatedTs": "2024-01-05T03:37:37",
"version": 11
}}


URI:/users/12/10002.json
Metadata: version = 12
Collections: v12, users, latest
{
"User": {
"id": "10002",
"firstName": "Amargo",
"lastName": "Leyburn",
"addresses": [
  {"address": {
   "line1": "123 State St.",
   "city": "Chicago",
   "state": "IL",
   "type": "Communication",
```

```
    "zip": "60164"
  }
}],
"updatedTs": "2024-01-09T05:23:17",
"version": 12
}}
```

In the above examples, a User document progresses from version 11 to version 12 due to changes in the address information. We record the version details in four locations.

1. As a document property (variant 1a)

2. As a metadata property (variant 1a)

3. In the URI (variant 1b)

4. As collections (variant 1c).

While using all these simultaneously is not mandatory, the choice depends on how we query versions. For instance, if the application primarily requires the latest versions and only occasionally accesses previous versions, optimizing queries for 'latest' collections may be a suitable approach. When there's a need for previous versions, we can direct queries to other collections.

There may be situations where incorporating version information into the document may conflict with information architecture principles, such as versions are not inherent to a business entity but are essential for persistence. This is where the Envelope Pattern becomes relevant as it introduces placeholders for information unrelated to the core entity, addressing concerns raised by information architects.

```
URI: /users/12/10002.json
Metadata: version = 11
Collections: v11, users
{"envelope": {
  "headers": {
    "version": 11
  },
  "instance": {
  "User": {
    "id": "1002",
    "firstName": "Amargo",
    "lastName": "Leyburn",
    "address": [
        {"Address": {
          "line1": "79859 Fairview Road",
          "city": "Brooklyn",
          "state": "NY",
          "type": "Communication",
          "zip": "11225"
          }
        }
    ],
    "updatedTs": "2024-01-05T03:37:37"
    }
  }
 }
}
```

Approaches to handle version details in the document, metadata, URI, or collection offer various implementation options:

Application-Driven Versioning

In this method, the application takes responsibility for determining the version and supplies this information through the API during data ingestion. The application side handles the entire version management implementation. This will, however, result in additional calls to the MarkLogic server for data. For example, the application-side logic will look something like this:

- Prepare the new content
- Open a transaction
- Query MarkLogic for the current latest version in the server
- Write back the current latest version back to the server as a previous version
- Write the new content as the new version
- Commit the transaction.

In-Database Versioning

The second approach involves determining version information within the database. When a document is ingested using Java/.NET client, REST client, or MLCP, we can invoke content transformation functions. These functions facilitate the necessary version management. The basic structure of a transform function might resemble this pseudo-code:

```
function myTransform (context, params, content)
{
// content.value has the new document
// context.uri has the new URI.
// Step 1:
// Query for the current latest version of
// the document.
// Step 2:
// Determine the version number of the
// document which is available in URI,
// collection, metadata or in content.
// Step 3:
// Re-insert the current document with a new URI.
// Ex.  If the latest version is maintained in
//   URI /users/<userId>.json in collection
//   "latest", assign the document to
```

```
//    /users/<version>/<userId>.json in
//    collection <version>.
// Step 4:
// Return content.  Now, the database should
// have the new content in identified by URI
// /users/<userId>.json in collection
// "latest".
return content;
}
export.transform = myTransform
```

The transformation function allows for the incorporation of intricate business logic to determine versions and reshape content as needed. It's essential to note that while transformation functions offer flexibility, they may introduce potential delays in the ingestion process due to additional business logic and I/O operations. In the previous approach, the same delay will be in the client application and not the database. If the version determination logic is straightforward, the impact on performance may be negligible. Therefore, early project planning during the design and modeling phase, where URI strategy and collection strategy are defined, becomes crucial to decide whether to retain previous versions of documents.

Trigger-Based Versioning

Variant 1d involves using database triggers. Conceptually, a trigger listens for specific events and then invokes a XQuery or JavaScript module after the event occurs. The trigger action module can run before or after committing the transaction, which causes the trigger to fire. For document versioning, a trigger responding to update events can perform the necessary updates to transition the current latest version to the previous version of the document. The implementation logic mirrors that of a transform function but is executed in response to an event and runs in the MarkLogic Task Server. For detailed examples, best practices, and configuration details of triggers, refer to the MarkLogic Server documentation.

The choice between these implementation methods depends on the specific use case and non-functional requirements. Benchmarking these options in a realistic environment can help determine the most suitable approach for a given situation.

Utilizing Temporal Documents

Variant 1e utilizes the Temporal Documents feature in MarkLogic, a specialized document management capability that stores documents as a series of versioned documents within a protected temporal collection. In this setup, the 'original' documents initially inserted into the database remain unchanged. Updates, including deletes to these documents, are added as "new" documents and are completed with metadata values indicating the time period during which the document is considered valid. Notably, we require no application or server code for this process.

For instance, upon the first insertion of a document into the temporal collection 'users' with the URI '/users/1002.json', the content remains unaltered. However, the collections assigned include 'users', 'latest', and '/users/1002. json'. Additionally, metadata values are as follows:

```
systemStart = <insertedDateTime>
systemEnd = 9999-12-31T11:59:59Z
```

For subsequent versions, the application code does not need to do anything for version management. The application simply continues inserting new document versions into the 'users' collection with the same URI '/users/1002.json'. MarkLogic automatically moves the prior current document to a new URI like '/users/1002.<randomNumber>.json'. The collections 'users' and '/users/1002.json' are updated, and metadata values change as follows:

```
systemStart = <the original insert time>
systemEnd = <the time when new version came in>
```

The new current document adopts the URI '/users/1002.json', with collections 'users', '/users/1002.json', and 'latest' assigned. Metadata values are updated as follows:

```
systemStart = <the time when new version came in>
systemEnd = 9999-12-31T11:59:59Z
```

In essence, application code remains oblivious to version management, as MarkLogic internally handles versions without any user-developed code. Should applications require access to old documents, built-in APIs are available for such operations.

It's important to note a few considerations regarding MarkLogic's temporal capability. Users can define the temporal collection (e.g., 'users') and the base URI (e.g., '/users/1002.json'). Developers can also define the tracked time axis, such as *systemStart* and *systemEnd*. However, MarkLogic determines the collection assignment of 'latest' and the pattern of versioned URIs, and the developer cannot control these. MarkLogic assumes that previous versions of documents are never deleted, and changing this default behavior requires additional administrative privileges. Additionally, versioning using temporal documents does not inherently include a *version number* concept unless managed by the application with custom logic. For more details and examples, refer to the MarkLogic Server documentation.

Utilizing Document Library Services

Variant 1f utilizes the Library Services feature of MarkLogic, which enables users to create and manage versioned content resembling the Content Management System (CMS) functionality. Access to managed documents follows a check-out/check-in model. When we initially place a document in MarkLogic under Library Services management, it creates version 1 of the document. Subsequent updates to the document result in creating new versions automatically. The retention of old versions is governed by a defined 'Retention Policy.'

The considerations of utilizing temporal documents apply here also. Like temporal documents, application code dictates the base URI, while Library Services internally manage the URIs. Additionally, Library

Services appends *properties* to the document (distinct from metadata used in temporal documents) containing version information. While user-controlled properties can be introduced, those added by Library Services remain unalterable. A notable distinction lies in the exposure of temporal features through Java APIs, built-in REST endpoints, and low-level XQuery/JavaScript APIs. In contrast, Library Services APIs lack direct REST or Java counterparts, necessitating the creation of custom REST extensions utilizing XQuery/JavaScript APIs for application development. For comprehensive details and examples, consult the MarkLogic Server documentation.

Variant 2 – Preserving only the differences between versions

This variant significantly diverges from the methods in variant 1. Unlike others, it doesn't retain the entire document but only the differences (deltas). While MarkLogic does not offer a built-in solution for this, it can adeptly manage this implementation. One direct approach involves using an in-bound transformation function, with the basic structure of such a transformation outlined as follows:

```
function myTransform (context, params, content) {
// content.value has the new document
// context.uri has the new URI.
// Step 1:
// Query for the current latest version of
// the document.
// Step 2:
// Find out all differences between the new
```

```
// document and the document already in
// database
// Step 3:
// Create a new document that has recorded
// the changes between the documents.
// Step 4:
// Return content.  Now, the database should
// have the new content in identified by URI
// /users/<userId>.json and another document
// that has changes extracted.
return content;
}
export.transform = myTransform
```

Alternatively, the implementation can reside within the client application. In such a scenario, the client application would execute a process akin to the following.

- Prepare the new content
- Open a transaction
- Query MarkLogic for the current latest version in the server
- Find out the differences between new content and the current latest version
- Write the changes as a new document to the server
- Write the new content to the server
- Commit the transaction.

Discovering variances between two multi-level XML or JSON documents may necessitate extensive coding, particularly when dealing with complexities such as repeated elements, embedded objects, and arrays.

Open-source libraries are available to streamline this process. The application code can define the structure of the change document, as illustrated in the example below, where a new address is appended to a user, and a phone number is modified.

```
{
  "changeTs": "2024-01-10T03:54:45. 890543Z",
  "key": "01GNCZZ8AF96XX6K8FN5BBFQQS",
  "changes": [
    {"kind": "ArrayChange",
     "path": ["address"],
     "index": 1,
     "item": {"kind": "New",
         "new": {
           "address": {
             "line1": "1345 State Street",
             "city": "Chicago",
             "state": "IL",
             "type": "Communication",
             "zip": "60164"
             }
           }}},
    {"kind": "Change",
     "path": ["communication",
         "Communication","phone"],
     "old": "2168674257",
     "new": "2168674260"
    }
  ]
}
```

We can present the change document created in a user interface:

	1	
Change Type	Update	
Change Time	2024-01-10T03:54:45.890543Z	
Change By	S6543	
Changes	Location	address
	Old Value	

	New Value	{
		"Address": {
		"line1": "1345 State Street",
		"city": "Chicago",
		"state": "IL",
		"type": "Communication",
		"zip": "60164"
		}}

	Location	communication.Communication.phone
	Old Value	2168674257
	New Value	2168674260

Figure 7.20: Document changes in a User Interface.

Applying the Document Versioning Pattern to our case study

The Document Versioning Pattern can fulfill the requirement of keeping track of any changes to the pet adoption certificates. Here is a sample adoption certificate document:

```
// an adoption Certificate document with
// Document Versioning
{
  "petId": "dog100666",
  "version": 1,
  "lastUpdateDt": "2023-01-06",
  "petName": "Cujo",
  "adoptionDt": "2023-01-08",
  "newOwners": [ "Steve King" ],
  "clauses": [
    "Adoption center will vaccinate dog for flu"
```

```
    ]
      .  .  .
}
```

The schema of the document appears in Figure 7.21.

petVersioning			
petId	pk	str	*
version		int	*
lastUpdateDt		date	*
petName		str	*
adoptionDt		str	
⊟ newOwners		arr	
[0]		str	
petStatus		str	
⊟ clauses		arr	
[0]		str	

Figure 7.21: Document Versioning Pattern Schema.

Then the new owners request to add Carrie, the family's daughter, as an owner on the certificate and convince the center to provide six months of special food for Cujo, who is just coming out of an illness. With these changes, the new version of the adoption certificate may look like this.

```
// an adoption Certificate document with
// Document Versioning
{
  "petId": "dog100666",
  "version": 2,
  "lastUpdateDt": "2023-01-07",
  "petName": "Cujo",
  "adoptionDt": "2023-01-08",
  "newOwners": [ "Steve King", "Carrie King"],
  "clauses": [
   "Adoption center will vaccinate dog for flu",
```

```
   "Adoption center will provide six months of
special dog food"
  ]
  . . .
}
```

The schema does not change due to this revision. All adoption certificates will be in a collection adoption_certificates. The latest certificate will also be in collection adoption_certificates_latest. From the system perspective, when the latest adoption certificate is required, the application will look in adoption_certificates_latest. When the historical versions are needed, they are available in adoption_certificates. The collection assignment can be done when the updates are done based on one of the implementation variations discussed before.

Benefits of Document Versioning Pattern

The Document Versioning Pattern is a great option when there is a need to keep track of changes to documents. It is not relatively easy to implement but avoids needing a dedicated version control system. The queries for the latest version of documents still perform well.

Trade-offs with the Document Versioning Pattern

Achieving the Document Versioning pattern is relatively straightforward, offering multiple implementation options with the possibility of significant automation. The queries for accessing the latest versions remain efficient and performant, as the latest versions are systematically stored in a distinct collection.

However, there are two notable drawbacks to this pattern. Firstly, it involves more write operations, which may become noteworthy when the frequency of changes is exceptionally high. Secondly, the overall database size increases due to the retention of full copies of previous versions. While maintaining complete versions facilitates easier comparison, it comes at the expense of increased storage space. The approach of 'Preserving only differences between two versions' addresses the concern of storage space but introduces a challenge – recreating the previous version of the document becomes intricate. Nonetheless, with careful resource planning, this pattern proves highly beneficial in scenarios where the significance of previous document versions is crucial.

Summary of the Document Versioning Pattern

Problem	• Need to keep older versions of the documents • Do not want to use a separate system (SCM or CMS) to keep track of a few document changes
Solution	• Use a field to track the version number of the document • User metadata to track version number • Use separate collections to keep the latest and older documents • User time to track changes • Store only changes
Use cases	• Financial applications • Insurance applications

	• Legal documents
	• Price or product description histories
Benefits	• Accomplish versioning of documents without separate system, still keeping the application performant
Trade-offs	• Increases the number of write operations
	• Frequent updates on large documents will consume more disk space

Table 7.12: The Document Versioning Pattern.

The Envelope Pattern

The motivation of the *Envelope Pattern* is to separate data intended for consumption from data intended for optimizing the efficiency and performance of the database. Said differently, it is useful to separate the data that is used to do something in MarkLogic from the business data used by the application or data services API.

There are several justifications for grouping envelope and payload in separate sections of a document:

- External ingested data may need to be stored as-is (unaltered), which may be the case for highly regulated environments

- Retain source data instead of leaving it behind in the transformation processes

- We must keep parts of the document in sync with legacy systems

- You need to standardize some data in a canonical form

- You may want a cleaner organization inside your documents

Description of the Envelope Pattern

The basic idea is to take your source data entity and make it a subdocument of a parent document. The parent document becomes the envelope for your source data. You then add additional sections that may contain metadata, lineage information, or transformed data as siblings within the envelope.

We can combine the Envelope Pattern with one or more patterns reviewed in this section, including the Schema Versioning Pattern and the Inheritance Pattern.

Implementing the Envelope Pattern

The example below shows the basic structure of the envelope.

```
{
 "envelope": {
   "header": { "This section contains metadata
(source
          descriptor, modification dates, tags
          etc.) and harmonized mappings of the
          instance data (canonical versions of the
          source filed data)."
          },
   "triples": { "This section contains semantic
triples
          generated during the harmonization
          process."
          },
   ""instance": { "This section contains the original
          data or the canonical representation
          of the data entity."
          },
   "attachments": { "This section preserves the
original
          source data for compliance and/or
          data governance."
          }
   }
}
```

The naming of each group is not particularly important, provided that it is consistent and meaningful to your organization. For example, instead of *envelope*, you could use the document type or data entity name. The *header* could be named *metadata*, whereas *instance* could also be called *data, payload,* or *source.*

```
// a document with an envelope for metadata
// separate from the data payload
{
  "envelope": {
    "header": {
      "schema_version": 4,
      "docRevision": 1,
      "creation_ts": "2023-03-01 15:15:15",
      "last_update_ts": "2023-03-01 15:15:15",
      "created_by": "jdoe",
      "provenance": {
         "source": "System A",
          "lineage": "map v0.1.3"
      }
      "harmonization": {
         "zipcode": "29466-0317",
      },
      "phone": "+1-555-444-7890"
    },
    "triples": [],
    "instance": { ... }
}
```

Figure 7.22 shows the schema for the above example. The metadata is grouped under a *header* subobject, while the data is in a *instance* subobject. The metadata in the *header* contains a subobject for lineage (provenance), a subobject for harmonization of data, and an array for semantic triples for defining relationships to other documents.

Figure 7.22: Envelope pattern schema example 1.

For example, we can use the harmonization section if data in this collection comes from different legacy systems. There could be a case when address data uses different field names for the same information, such as zip, postcode, and postal_code. We assume here that there's a good reason to keep the field names in their original version. Hence, we are using a harmonization section to ensure compatibility.

MarkLogic Data Hub[19] is an open-source software interface that works to ingest data from multiple sources, harmonize the data, master it into a MarkLogic database, and then expose the data via data services. Data Hub uses the Envelope Pattern extensively and automatically creates *enveloped* documents in the structure mentioned above.

Applying the Envelope Pattern to our case study

Applying the Envelope Pattern is very easy, and we can combine it with all the other schema design patterns covered in this section. The only difficulty might be migrating to this pattern if you did not adopt it initially. With our Pet system, as originally imagined, data has been coming from a single Access database. But we can imagine that business has been booming, and our animal shelter has acquired a competitor across town. We now have to integrate data from multiple systems, and of course, different naming conventions and formats have been used. During the transition period, we must ensure compatibility with the different systems.

```
// a document coming from the animal
// shelter's Access database
{
 "envelope": {
   "header": {
     "docURI": "/birds/102345.json"
     "schema_version": 2,
     "docRevision": 1,
```

---

[19] MarkLogic Data Hub, https://www.marklogic.com/solutions/architectures/data-hub.

```
        "creation_ts": "2023-03-01 15:15:15",
        "last_update_ts": "2023-03-01 15:15:15",
        "created_by": " John Smith ",
        "provenance": {
            "source": "MS-Access",
                "lineage": " map v0.2.2"
            },
            "harmonization": {
                "zipcode": "74866-3457",
                "phone": "+1-555-444-7890"
            }
        },
        "triples": [],
        "instance": {
            "new_owner": "Steve King",
            "phoneNumber": "555-444-7890",
            "full_address": {
                "houseNum": "74866",
                "street": "123 Main Street",
                "box": "Apt. 749",
                "city": "Anytown",
                "state": "CA",
                "zip": "29466-0317"
            }
        }
    }
  }
}
```

The schema for the above documents appears in Figure 7.23. You will notice that this Envelope Pattern example also uses the Schema Versioning Pattern and the Inheritance Pattern to accommodate the different structures of the two source systems. With Hackolade Studio, you can prefill each new document schema in your model with the structure of your choice using the Snippets functionality.

Figure 7.23: Envelope pattern schema example 2.

Benefits of the Envelope Pattern

Separating metadata from the payload can help with the efficiency and accuracy of queries and other database operations. This is achieved by harmonizing data coming from different systems at the time of document creation so we can trust each query to return accurate results without altering data that might be necessary for legacy systems.

The Envelope Pattern also brings consistency to a model between different entities. For example, whether it is Order, Customer, or Product, the instance will be at envelope -> instance -> <Order, Customer, Product>.

Trade-offs with the Envelope Pattern

The additional metadata in the envelope can add some complexity to the data model and APIs. Depending on the application, the benefits might be minimal and not worth the complexity.

In some circumstances, separating the metadata from the payload may actually make queries less efficient, for example, if the metadata needs to be joined with the payload to produce the expected result.

The attachments section of the envelope might contribute largely to the document size. For example, a document with 10,000 elements is ingested. If there is interest in only 100 of the elements, the Envelope Pattern lets you move the 100 elements to the instance section and leave 10,000 elements in the attachments section. The document size will be the total of everything in the envelope. Remember that MarkLogic will index all the content in the document. This can be useful if there is no *dark data* or *hidden data,* but we should consider the ramifications on document size.

Summary of the Envelope Pattern

Problem	• Data stored with different structures must be queried in a uniform manner
Solution	• Separate data intended for consumption (the "payload"), from data intended to optimize the power and flexibility of the database and application (the "envelope")
Use cases	• Data lineage • Integration of data coming from different legacy systems
Benefits	• Improve the efficiency and accuracy of queries by harmonizing data at document creation time • Improve legibility and understanding of documents by grouping metadata and data payload separately
Trade-offs	• Increased complexity of document structure and APIs • Potentially makes queries less efficient if metadata must be joined with the payload • Increases the overall size of the document

Table 7.13: The Envelope Pattern.

The Extended Reference Pattern

Even if you migrated from ten tables in a relational database to a few collections in MarkLogic, you may still encounter situations where you need to perform queries involving the joining of data from various documents. There are also situations where it makes sense to have separate things/entities as we have already seen in the *Embedding versus Referencing* topic.

We should be mindful that the join operation is not native to the MarkLogic document model. While it is possible to perform join operations using URIs, semantic RDF triples, or JavaScript/XQuery Optic APIs, MarkLogic is not necessarily optimized for joining documents. The Extended Reference Pattern focuses on how to minimize joins, thus making the reads faster. Before understanding this pattern, it is important to read the section *Embedding versus Referencing*, which describes the factors to consider before deciding whether to embed or reference.

Description of the Extended Reference Pattern

The Extended Reference Pattern is an alternate solution between embedding and referencing another document. It embeds the frequently used section of the document to avoid doing joins for important queries. It also keeps a complete version of the document in another location, referencing it when we need more information.

This pattern helps meet performance requirements for many applications. For example, the end user UI application first lists the customers with only minimal information about each customer, such as first name, last name, email address, and phone number. But the complete details of the customer are available when you click on the *View Details* button. In such a use case, the information that should be displayed in the initial screen should be displayed to the user fast, which can be accomplished if avoiding the join with other documents. When we click the *View Details* button, we can obtain the remaining information about the customer by joining the customer document with other related documents like orders. This join will be much faster because we can build the queries with very specific criteria like a customer id.

When choosing which fields to augment the reference information, opt for those that do not or rarely change. In the example above, the core details of customer rarely change. Hence, these fields are good candidates to duplicate from the customer details document to the customer document. The primary objective is to show the initial listing screen quickly for a good user experience.

There are several examples where we can apply the Extended Reference Pattern. In a Movie and Movie Details example, fields such as genre and release date are good candidates for Movie Details to copy over to Movie. Similarly, in the case of Customers and Orders, the customer's name, address, and phone number are good candidates to copy from the Customer document to the Order document.

Hackolade describes this concept of bringing additional fields from one entity to another as a *Foreign Master* in Hackolade Studio. The tool also reflects the information in the Document Relationship Diagrams.

Implementing the Extended Reference Pattern

To implement the Extended Reference Pattern, take the following steps:

- Identify frequent queries where it is possible to avoid joins. This will often require a clear understanding of the end-user applications, especially about how the data is used and the performance requirements. Copy the fields from the references into the main document.

- Update the source code to update the main document and the references as required.

Applying the Extended Reference Pattern to our case study

In our original model for the Pet Adoption application, we store the reference to the breed codes and the breed names for a given pet. Similarly, we do the same for the colors and vaccinations. These four pieces of information are all examples of using the Extended Reference Pattern.

The purpose of storing the code and the name is two-fold. When displaying a pet, we also want to show the breed list. If we only maintain the breed code in the pet document, we must join the breed documents to the pet document for the complete breed list. MarkLogic allows such joins, but as in many database technologies, joins are expensive, and we must avoid them for a system to perform well. So, instead of only storing the reference to the other document, we include the most frequently used information. In this case, the *breed name*. The breed code is still helpful for pulling more information about the breed if a user requests it by clicking on the *breed name*. In other words, as described earlier, copy in the fields for frequent queries to avoid performing joins, especially for queries that provide a list of pets.

```
// a Breed document
{
  "breedId": "breed101",
  "breedName": "Dalmatian",
  "breedOrigin": "Croatia",
  "breedTraits": [
    "loyal to the family",
    "good with children",
    . . .
  ],
  . . .
}

// a Pet document
{
  "petId": "dog19370824",
  "petName": "Fanny",
  "breeds": [
    {
      "code": "breed101",
      "name": "Dalmatian"
    }
  ]
}
```

The schema of the above documents appears in Figure 7.24.

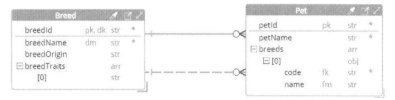

Figure 7.24: Extended Reference Pattern schema example.

If the *breed name* is immutable, then this pattern works the best. However, if the system goes through situations like renaming a breed, the system should also rename the breed names we duplicated in the pet document. That will introduce some implementation complexity on the application side. The pseudo-code for this will be:

- Begin transaction
- Update Breed document
- If Breed Name is changed
    - Get all Pet documents having the same breed code
    - Update all the matching Pet documents
- Commit transaction

We can manage this transaction from the client application, such as Java, or within a server code implemented in JavaScript or XQuery.

Benefits of the Extended Reference Pattern

Because the Extended Reference Pattern represents a pre-joined relationship, reads will be faster. There is no need to read multiple documents and join them for the final response. When we do not use the Extended Reference Pattern, we would either use Optic queries to read documents from different collections and return the joined documents through /v1/rows REST endpoint or as a data service.

Trade-offs with the Extended Reference Pattern

Maintaining more information than a simple reference to another object means we will duplicate information. This duplication comes at a cost, but this cost can be minimal if the additional fields are not mutable values. Also, when to copy the fields is an important consideration. The business logic to identify and copy the fields could result in slow ingest. We can use all of the methods mentioned in the *Embedding versus Referencing* section to copy the fields. Another consideration to make is keeping duplicate information up-to-date. In the pet example, if the name changes in the breed document, the breed names duplicated in the pet documents should also change to ensure data quality, adding more complexity to the updates. A thoughtful selection of which information to duplicate can handle the complexity better.

Summary of the Extended Reference Pattern

The *Extended Reference Pattern* is a good solution when both embedding and referencing are not optimal. It works well for modeling many-to-many relationships.

Problem	• Too many joins in read operations
	• Embedding leads to documents that are too big
Solution	• Identify fields using joins for the most common read operations
	• Copy these fields as an embedded subdocument in the main document
Use cases	• Catalog
	• Mobile applications
	• Real-time analytics
Benefits	• Faster reads
	• Lesser number of joins and lookups
Trade-offs	• Potentially creates data duplication
	• Could result in additional complexity in handling updates

Table 7.14: The Extended Reference Pattern

The Polymorphic Pattern

The Polymorphic Pattern is applied when documents share more similarities than differences. This pattern is particularly suitable for scenarios where querying documents despite their variations is essential, such as to provide a comprehensive 360-degree view of an entity like a Customer.

Description of the Polymorphic Pattern

Let's begin by revisiting the concept of Polymorphism in Object-Oriented Programming. Poly (many) - morph (change or form) - ism denotes situations where something takes on various forms. In the context of entities or documents, polymorphism refers to a scenario where documents within a collection are similar but not identical. This is a prevalent scenario encountered across various industries and contexts. For instance, an insurance company issuing both Auto and Home insurance policies may possess policy documents that vary in coverages, assets, and liabilities, yet share common information such as household details, forms, and payment options. Similar situations may arise during systems integration post-acquisition or when consolidating data from diverse sources.

```
{"Person": {
"firstName": "Earl",
"middleName": "I",
"lastName": "Anthony",
"type": "employee",
"active" : true,
....
"Details": {
        "designation": "Data Scientist",
        "department": "Business Intelligence",
        "managerId": 10042,
        "joinDt": "2024-01-10",
        "terminationDt": null,
        "employeeId": 90002
        ....
}}}
```

```
{"Person": {
"firstName": "Blair",
"middleName": "",
"lastName": "McGarel",
"type": "customer",
"active": true,
....
"Details": {
        "occupation": "Realtor",
        "joinDt": "2021-11-10",
        "customerId": "C720002"
        ....
}}}
```

Shared / Common attributes

Figure 7.25: Common attributes.

Implementing the Polymorphic Pattern

To implement the Polymorphism Pattern, follow these steps

- Identify entities that logically or business-wise should be grouped together in one collection.

- Utilize MarkLogic's feature to support one document assigned to multiple collections; make sure additional collections are also identified. For instance, in the context of Auto and Home policies, Auto Policy documents can reside in both *Policy* and *AutoPolicy* collections, while Home Policy documents can be in *Policy* and *HomePolicy* collections. This enables queries for all policies to target the *Policy* collection, while queries specific to Auto Policies can focus on the *AutoPolicy* collection.

- Identify common fields across these objects and model these fields at the root of the document.

- Identify fields that differ based on type and model these fields in sub-documents (embedded objects).

- Ensure that there is an attribute (e.g., type) that identifies the entity.

- Identify the necessary special indexes for faster queries. All these indexes may not get identified during the modeling or design phase; they can be built when queries are profiled and tested.

Applying the Polymorphic Pattern to our case study

In our Pet Adoption use case, we want the capability to query information about celebrity status, adoption details, etc., for all birds, cats, and dogs. To facilitate this, the Pet collection incorporates the Polymorphism Pattern, encompassing different yet similar objects: Birds, Cats, and Dogs. Additionally, a *petType* field is introduced, and the specific fields of each pet type are organized into a subobject. Here are sample documents for each pet type:

```
// a Pet document for a bird
{
  "petId": "bird102345",
  "petName": "Birdie",
  "petTyoe": "bird",
  ...
  "bird": {
    "exoticIndicator": false
  }
},
// a Pet document for a cat
{
  "petId": "cat108545",
  "petName": "Tiger",
  "petType": "cat",
  ...
  "cat": {
    "deClawedIndicator": false
  }
},
// a Pet document for a dog
{
  "petId": "dog102345",
  "petName": "Rex",
  "petType": "dog",
  ...
  "dog": {
    "childFriendlyIndicator": true
  }
},
```

Figure 7.26 shows the schema for the above documents. In the implementation phase, we include all these documents in a *pets* collection. Each document will also be assigned one of the *birds*, *cats*, or *dogs* collections based on the *petType*. Queries needing information for all pets will be executed against *pets* collection. For specific queries targeting only birds, we confine the search to the *birds* collection, and similarly for *cats* and *dogs*.

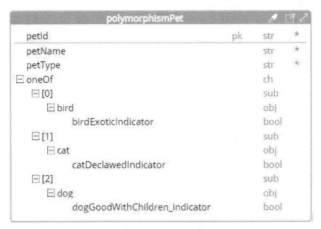

Figure 7.26: Schema for the above documents.

Benefits of the Polymorphic Pattern

Implementing the Polymorphism pattern is straightforward, making it developer-friendly and user-friendly. Composing search queries is simplified as queries only need to reference a single collection, eliminating the need for joins. This leads to faster application development. Additionally, the flexibility of assigning multiple collections to a document allows the creation of more precise and targeted queries.

Trade-offs with the Polymorphic Pattern

There are minimal considerations to be aware of. As mentioned earlier, the selection of indexes can be somewhat intricate. For instance, if you specifically need to index the join date of only employees and not

customers, the path range index would be
/Person[type="employee"]/Details/joinDt . If the
type="employee" condition is not there, join Dates of
customer documents will also be indexed, consuming
more resources.

Summary of the Polymorphic Pattern

Problem	<ul><li>Documents are more similar than different</li><li>Need to query the documents on their similitudes</li></ul>
Solution	<ul><li>Keep documents in a single collection</li><li>Use a field to identify the document type</li><li>Optionally, use a structure for commonalities and another for differences</li></ul>
Use cases	<ul><li>Single View</li><li>Product Catalog</li><li>Content Management</li></ul>
Benefits	<ul><li>Easy to implement</li><li>Allow querying across a single collection</li></ul>
Trade-offs	<ul><li>Indexes need to be defined carefully</li></ul>

Table 7.15: The Polymorphic Pattern.

The Schema Versioning Pattern

Data is always changing over time. As business and technical requirements evolve, so does the structure of your data. This impacts applications that must evolve to support these new and changing requirements. Thus, incorporating schema changes, including adding data elements or modifying existing ones, becomes inevitable.

MarkLogic adopts a schema-agnostic approach while not being completely schema-free. There are no schema rules beyond syntax requirements in a schema-free database, making proper JSON or XML acceptable. However, a schema-free database lacks a mechanism to enforce good structure rules for the data, potentially leading to a decline in data quality over time. In such databases, the responsibility for ensuring data conformity to a schema rests solely on the applications generating the data.

In contrast, MarkLogic is not bound by a schema but remains aware of schemas. This means that it is feasible if there is a desire to enforce a schema at the database level. MarkLogic does not mandate the adoption of a schema, but if one (or more) is in place, it can be enforced. Schema awareness plays a crucial role in data governance and the maintenance of data quality.

The Schema Versioning Pattern provides a solution of maintaining awareness of schema in a schema-agnostic environment, supporting upgrades and changes as the application evolves.

Description of the Schema Versioning Pattern

The Schema Versioning Pattern establishes a structure within documents to facilitate seamless schema upgrades. This straightforward pattern ensures that applications can identify the schema version of the document they are processing and eliminates the need for application downtime during upgrades.

Additionally, it also provides a mechanism to implement a capability to read a document through a version upgrade or downgrade process. The pattern also supports bulk conversion of documents from one schema version to another. Regardless, we must prepare the data consumer applications to handle the new schema to ensure a smooth transition.

The Schema Versioning Pattern simply involves maintaining a schema version number for each document. As discussed with many other patterns, this version number can be located in one or more of the following places:

- Embedded as a property or element within the JSON or XML document. In this approach, the version information becomes part of the business entity.

- If we also use the Envelope Pattern, it can be placed in the 'headers' section of the envelope, ensuring the business entity remains unaffected.

- As a name-value pair information in the metadata of the document. In this case, the version information will not be part of the document content, but only in metadata. During writing and reading documents, metadata needs to be specifically updated and read to manage the version information.

The choice between these options primarily depends on the information architect's modeling practices, specifically whether the version number is considered part of the business entity.

The Schema Versioning Pattern can provide benefits in addressing various implementation scenarios that may arise during schema upgrades:

- **Matching versions for producer and consumer applications**. The ideal scenario involves alignment between the documents in the database and the applications that require them, ensuring both comprehend the same version. For instance, at the initiation of the schema, producers generate data adhering to schema version 1. The database then stores this version, and consumers are designed to understand only schema version 1. In the event of a schema version upgrade to version 2, producers generate data in accordance with the new schema, pre-existing documents in the database are converted to version 2, and all consumers are concurrently prepared to accept and process data in version 2 of the schema.

- **Lower version requirement for consumer applications**. This occurs when applications in a higher version generate documents, but the consuming applications are not yet prepared to handle that version.

- **Higher version requirement for consumer applications**. Arises when consumer applications are already upgraded to read higher versions, but there are pre-existing documents in the database in the lower version.

Bulk upgrade of documents to a higher version occurs when all applications reading the documents are updated to handle the new version, and all applications writing the documents are producing the new version. In this case, we can upgrade all existing documents in the database to conform to the new schemas.

These scenarios arise due to the complexities of the application landscape, where aligning all schema upgrades, updates to pre-existing documents, and application upgrades to accommodate schema changes simultaneously is challenging. In an ideal world, these upgrades would occur concurrently. However, in a complex application environment with diverse priorities, achieving alignment at the same time becomes difficult. Undertaking such a schema change as a single program could result in the slowest team involved determining the program's delivery speed.

Implementing the Schema Versioning Pattern

To handle all the scenarios mentioned above, a field is needed at the core to store the schema version (Ex. schemaVersionNum). The steps in implementing the pattern are:

- Add a `schemaVersionNum` field to the documents

- Change the application code to write the correct version number to the documents

- If needed, build an outbound transform function to convert the documents from one version to another version.

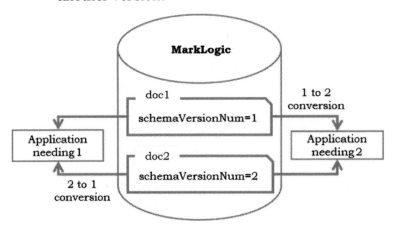

Figure 7.27: Version Conversions using transforms.

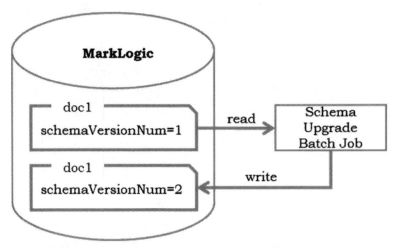

Figure 7.28: Schema Upgrades through a batch job.

For bulk migration, develop application code (or tools like CORB2[20]) to convert pre-existing documents to a newer version. As part of the migration, the schemaVersionNum increases to a higher number.

Schema Validations

To ensure data quality in a schema-agnostic database like MarkLogic, the documents should be able to be validated against a schema. MarkLogic provides built-in APIs to validate the documents against a pre-defined schema.

Table **7.16** contains some APIs available in MarkLogic for validating the schemas. For usage and examples, refer to MarkLogic documentation.

JavaScript	XQuery
xdmp.jsonValidate	xdmp:json-validate
xdmp.jsonValidateNode	xdmp:json-validate-node
xdmp.jsonValidateReport	xdmp:json-validate-report
xdmp.jsonValidateReportNode	xdmp:json-validate-report-node
schematron.validate	schematron:validate
xdmp.validate	xdmp:validate

Table 7.16: APIs available for validating the schemas.

A suitable API can be employed within the application to verify whether the document aligns with the anticipated schema. As these validations might potentially increase the overall response time of the application, it is advisable to selectively enable them based on conditions,

---

[20] https://developer.marklogic.com/code/corb/.

such as enabling only in a test environment or when in *debug* mode. We can also involve these validation APIs through triggers and log the output from the validation API for subsequent analysis and actions.

Applying the Schema Versioning Pattern to our case study

Illustrating the application of the Schema Versioning Pattern in the context of the pet adoption use case is straightforward, as mentioned earlier. From a modeling perspective, the minimum requirement is to include the schemaVersionNum in the Pet document. The necessary operations for schema migrations are to be implemented in transforms (for temporary migrations) or within the application code. The primary objective of the pattern is to ensure that the reading application is aware of the schema to which the document conforms.

In the pet adoption use case, let us assume that the versions required by applications align with the version specified in the document. Additionally, let us consider a scenario where the original model did not contemplate consolidating all attributes under a single property. Here is a sample of the initial version of the document:

```
// a Pet document with a schema version before
// migration
{
  "petId": "bird102345",
  "schemaVersionNum": 1,
  "petName": "Lady G",
  "breeds": [ "Nightingale" ],
  "traits":
```

```
  [ "Found mostly in Europe",
    "European Robin",
    "Best singing bird" ],
  "colors": [ "brown", "white"]
}
```

Figure 7.29: Schema Versioning Pattern example.

Upon considering the incorporation of breeds, traits, and colors as searchable attributes that should be organized under a subdocument named *searchAttributes*, the sample document is structured as follows:

```
// a Pet document with a schema version after
// migration
{ "petId": "bird102345",
  "schemaVersionNum": 2,
  "petName": "Lady G",
  "searchAttributes": {
      "breeds": [ "Nightingale" ],
"traits":
    [ "Found mostly in Europe",
      "European Robin",
      "Best singing bird" ],
"colors": [ "brown", "white"]
}}
```

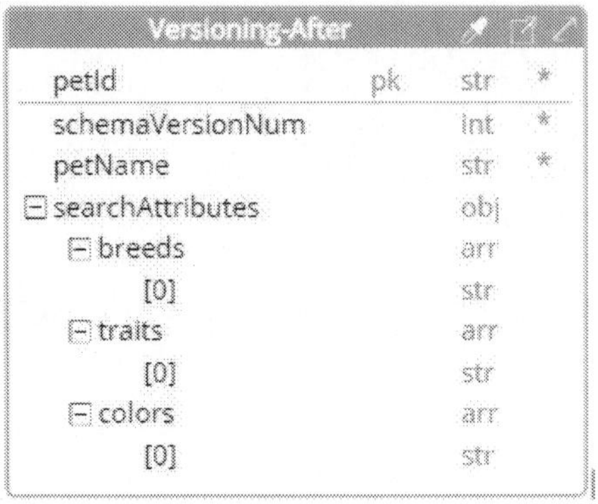

Figure 7.30: Schema Versioning Pattern example.

When reading the document, the application code should be able to discern the version to which the document adheres and follow the appropriate logic path accordingly.

Benefits of the Schema Versioning Pattern

By engaging in thoughtful modeling upfront, we can streamline the necessary application changes to accommodate schemas. The primary advantage of this pattern lies in its ability to upgrade schemas with flexibility, all without requiring application downtime.

Trade-offs with the Schema Versioning Pattern

In cases where version conversion occurs during document read, the response time encompasses the conversion process, even if it is minimal. To mitigate this, one approach is to plan changes across all applications simultaneously. When simultaneous changes are not feasible, planning and allocating resources to handle the conversion efficiently is advisable. An alternative option is for applications to read multiple versions through separate queries and subsequently join the results within the application code. It is essential to emphasize that the pattern's primary goal is to ensure that the application comprehends the version of the schema to which the document conforms.

It's common to distinguish between major and minor schema version changes. Minor changes, even if not all applications are simultaneously ready, typically result in less complex conversions during read, minimizing the impact on performance. Major changes require careful planning—a coordinated cut-over where all applications transition to the new schema simultaneously.

Summary of the Schema Versioning Pattern

Problem	• A framework to do schema upgrades without downtime
Solution	• Add schema version to document
	• Modify application code to handle schema variants
	• Progressively update documents
Use cases	• Applicable to all use cases, especially when there is no tolerance for downtimes
Benefits	• Schema migration without downtime
Trade-offs	• Temporary complexity when schema variants exist

Table 7.17: The Schema Versioning Pattern.

The Subset Pattern

Consider a scenario where a phone book is extracted from a source system and transmitted to your system. The phone book may resemble one of the following examples:

```
{[ {"Person": {
      "id": 1001,
      "firstName": "Tom",
      "lastName": "Jacob",
      "Address": { ... },
      "Communication": {...}
    }
  },
  {"Person": {
      "id": 1002,
      "firstName": "Tom",
      "lastName": "Jacob",
      "Address": {...},
      "Communication": {...}
    }
  }
 ]
}

<root>
    <Person>
        <id>1001</id>
        <firstName>Tom</firstName>
        <lastName>Jacob</lastName>
        <Address>...</Address>
        <Communication>...</Communication>
    </Person>
    <Person>
        <id>1002</id>
        <firstName>Tom</firstName>
        <lastName>Jacob</lastName>
        <Address>...</Address>
        <Communication>...</Communication>
    </Person>
</root>
```

In the instances above, there are recurring "Person" elements, each representing an individual entity. In many business application scenarios, each "Person" entity should be handled separately for display or updates.

Another scenario arises when documents contain numerous related entities. In the examples provided, there's a sizable "Product" entity accompanied by several "Review" entities.

```
{ "Product": {
    "sku": 10001,
    "name": "myProduct",
    "reviews": [
      { "Review": {
          "id": "399343133",
          "text": "myFirstReview"
        }
      },
      { "Review": {
          "id": "5233482683",
          "text": "mySecondReview"
        }}
    ]
  }}
```

```
<Product>
  <sku>10001</sku>
  <name>myProduct</name>
  <reviews>
    <Review>
      <id>399343133</id>
      <text>myFirstReview</text>
    </Review>
    <Review>
      <id>5233482683</id>
      <text>mySecondReview</text>
    </Review>
  </reviews>
</Product>
```

Over time, the number of reviews a product receives could reach into the thousands. Typically, only the most recent reviews are relevant for display alongside the product. What these scenarios share is the need for the application to access only specific sections of the larger document. In both situations, the challenge lies in the potential for documents to expand significantly, potentially surpassing the recommended size limit for MarkLogic. The optimal document size in MarkLogic is typically around 100K or slightly larger. It's important to note that while the documents in the provided examples are large, the focus at any given moment is often on a specific section rather than the entirety of the document.

The Subset pattern proves valuable in applications dealing with very large documents, where the need is to concentrate on a portion of the overall content.

Description of the Subset Pattern

At the heart of the Subset Pattern lies the extraction of specific information from a larger document and its placement into related documents. This extraction process may entail some degree of data duplication, making the pattern particularly suitable for scenarios where such duplication is acceptable or even desirable.

For instance, consider product reviews or completed bank transactions, which typically cannot be altered once submitted or executed. In such cases, duplicating the most recent ten reviews or transactions alongside the corresponding Product or Account entity should not present an issue. Conversely, it may enhance the user experience by providing readily accessible information.

In essence, the Subset Pattern offers a methodical approach to organizing and presenting relevant data segments, optimizing usability and efficiency within various applications.

There are two variations of Subset pattern:

- Splitting a one-to-many relationship
- Splitting a document
    - Breaking down a large document into a set of smaller documents and having a one-to-one relationship between the set.
    - Restricting an array to a subset of elements

The primary motivation for employing this pattern stems from potential conflicts with three existing design principles:

- Grouping together related information.
- Accessing only the necessary information.
- Minimizing the use of joins.

Variant A - Splitting a one-to-many relationship

To demonstrate the application of this variant, let's consider our product and reviews scenario. A very appealing modeling technique is to embed all reviews pertaining to that product in the product document itself. However, this design presents a challenge: if there are numerous reviews, the document becomes unwieldy.

Moreover, it risks violating the principle of "Read only the information that we need," as most users won't read every review.

An alternative approach is to store each review in a separate document and then aggregate them with the product information at query time. However, this introduces the problem of violating the guideline against minimizing joins.

Practically, customers may only be interested in a subset of reviews, reducing the necessity to fetch all reviews every time. The optimal solution lies somewhere between embedding everything and referencing everything.

In many cases, moderate solutions tend to be more effective than extreme positions. With this understanding, we can devise a balanced approach by limiting the number of reviews in the product document to perhaps 5, 10, 20, or another number that caters to most users. The selection criteria for these reviews could be based on recency or popularity, depending on what suits our application best.

Variant B - Splitting a document

Another scenario where splitting a larger document is highly beneficial is when the incoming document is an aggregation of records. This commonly occurs with daily transaction feeds or comprehensive phone books listing all customers. Handling such documents as single entities can lead to significant inefficiencies due to their immense size.

For instance, consider a phone book containing one million customers stored as a single JSON array or XML document with repeating elements. Searching for or updating information about a single customer would technically involve processing a document containing all one million entries. This approach is inherently inefficient.

A more efficient strategy involves breaking down the large document into smaller, more manageable units. By doing so, tasks such as searching and updating information become significantly more performant and less resource-intensive.

Implementing the Subset Pattern

To implement the Subset Pattern, take these steps:

- Identify the array, the one-to-many relationship, or the set of fields to divide

- Identify the rule for selecting documents to place in the main document

- Create a script to split the documents and assign to correct collection(s). In MarkLogic, a couple of ways exist.

  - MarkLogic Content Pump (MLCP) is a command line utility that can used to disaggregate large XML files with aggregate data into multiple smaller documents rooted at a recurring element.

- o In bound transform functions written in JavaScript, XSLT or XQuery can be used to split XML and JSON documents into multiple documents.

- Schedule the invocation of the script as needed by your use case.

Applying the Subset Pattern to our case study

To illustrate the Subset Pattern, remember that one of our requirements for our Pet Adoption application was to let interested customers see a few comments regarding the pet's breed on its main page.

Again, to avoid doing a costly join to the comments for that breed, we bring the top three comments for the breed into each pet's document. Documents in the breedComments collection may look like the following:

```
// breed comment documents
{
  "id": "9001",
  "breedId": "breed101",
  "breedName": "Dalmatian",
  "commentRank": 1,
  "comment":
    "I owned ten Dalmatians over the years \
    and this breed is the most loyal breed \
    I have ever encountered.          \
    Nevertheless, these dogs don't see  \
    themselves as dogs but as members of \
    the family, with the same rights."
```

```
    },
    {
      "id": "9002",
      "breedId": "breed101",
      "breedName": "Dalmatian",
      "commentRank": 2,
      "comment":
        "The one thing to know about Dalmatians   \
        is that they are subject to many illnesses \
        like deafness and kidney stones. Don't    \
        expect them to live as long as other      \
        breeds."
    },
    {
      "id": "9003",
      "breedId": "breed101",
      "breedName": "Dalmatian",
      "commentRank": 3,
      "comment":
        "This is a very stubborn breed of dog.    \
        Expect to spend time training them.       \
        If you are not ready for this commitment, \
        you should choose another breed."
    },
    ...
```

Figure 7.31 shows the schema for the above documents.

Figure 7.31: Subset pattern breed schema.

Applying the *Subset Pattern*, we bring the top three rated comments into each pet document.

```
// a Pet document
{
  "id": "dog19370824",
  "name": "Fanny",
  "breeds": [
    {
      "code": "breed101",
      "name": "Dalmatian",
      "topComments": [
    "I owned ten Dalmatians over the years \
    and this breed is the most loyal breed \
    I have ever encountered.  Nevertheless, \
    these dogs don't see themselves as dogs \
    but as members of the family, with the \
    same rights.",                          \
    "The one thing to know about Dalmatians  \
    is that they are subject to many illnesses \
    like deafness and kidney stones.  Don't  \
    expect them to live as long as other \
    breeds.",
    "This is a very stubborn breed of dog.  \
    Expect to spend time training them.     \
    If you are not ready for this commitment, \
    you should choose another breed."
      ]
    }
  ],
}
```

Figure 7.32 shows the schema for the above documents.

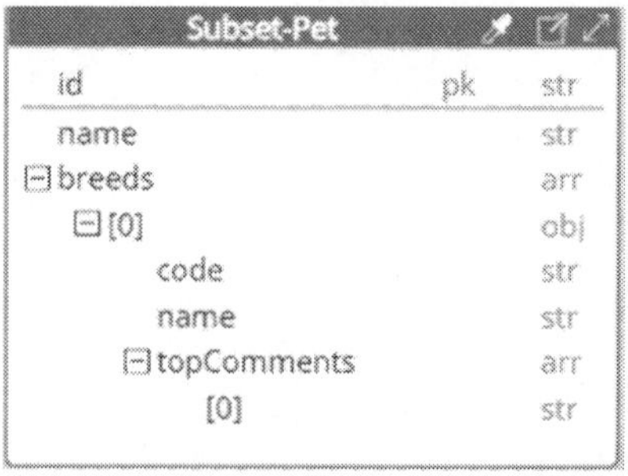

Figure 7.32: Subset Pattern pet schema.

As discussed earlier, the Subset Pattern introduced data duplication. In this case, there is little of an impact. The comments in this pet document don't have to be in sync all the time with the ones from the `breedComments` collection. A periodic job can adjust the comments.

Benefits of the Subset Pattern

1. Reduced Memory Footprint: By selectively loading only the necessary subset of data into memory, this pattern helps minimize the size of the working set. This efficient memory usage is crucial for systems with limited resources or dealing with large datasets.

2. Improved Loading Speed: Since the document contains precisely what is required and nothing more, it can be loaded quickly. This results in lower latency, which is particularly advantageous for user-facing applications where responsiveness is key to providing a seamless user experience.

3. Optimized Performance: By avoiding the unnecessary loading of excess information, the Subset Pattern contributes to optimized system performance. This optimization is essential for applications handling high volumes of data or requiring rapid data access and processing.

Overall, the Subset Pattern's focus on selective data loading leads to enhanced efficiency, reduced latency, and improved performance across various applications and systems.

Trade-offs with the Subset Pattern

The only shortcoming of Subset pattern is the possibility data duplication as the most needed related information is kept with the original document. As discussed earlier, the impact of data duplication should be considered before choosing this pattern.

Summary of the Subset Pattern

The Subset Pattern helps reduce the amount of RAM consumed by the system. We split the information between what needs to be accessed immediately and what can be accessed by a subsequent request.

Problem	• Large documents are taking up a lot of space in memory
Solution	• Break up arrays of subdocuments to only keep a minimum number of elements all the time • Migrate the remaining documents to a second collection
Use cases	• List of reviews • List of comments • A long list of nearly anything kept in an array
Benefits	• Smaller documents with shorter load time • Smaller working set in memory
Trade-offs	• Potentially creates data duplication

Table 7.18: The Subset Pattern.

The Semantic Graph Pattern

In a relational data model, the context of data is often inferred mainly by the structure (table) in which the data attributes reside and the relationships with other entities. With a semantic data model (SDM), the approach is to design data structures that focus on capturing the meaning and relationships between data attributes. It goes beyond traditional relational modeling techniques by incorporating the semantics or meaning of the data into the design.

Description of the Semantic Graph Pattern

The Resource Description Framework (RDF)[21] is the foundation for the semantic data model. Recall from our discussion on data model types, RDF graph consists of three simple components: a subject, a predicate, and an object. For this reason, it is often referred to as RDF triples. For example, "The sky has the color blue" consists of a subject (*the sky*), a predicate (*has color*), and an object (*blue*). We can understand this triple model as like the classical entity-attribute-value model.

The semantic data model aligns well with this book's Align, Refine, and Design theme. At the align level, semantic modeling involves identifying a given domain's key concepts or entities. We also define the relationships between concepts, identifying associations, dependencies, and hierarchies between them. Concepts can be anything from traditional customers, orders, and

---

[21] https://en.wikipedia.org/wiki/Resource_Description_Framework.

products to more abstract things like transactions or events. Since RDF triples are directional, describing more than one relationship between concepts is possible. A revised business term model using triples appears in Figure 7.33.

Using the techniques prescribed in the Refine section, you add more detail to the conceptual SDM by adding new concepts/entities along with related triples or further defining existing concepts/entities, properties, data types, and constraints. Finally, at the Design level, MarkLogic provides two variants for implementing a semantic data model, which we will discuss in more detail shortly.

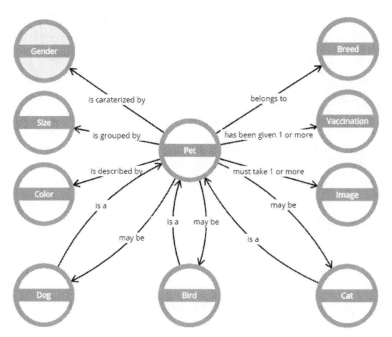

Figure 7.33: A revised Business Term Model using triples.

Since triples can be linked (the object of one triple becomes the subject of another triple), they form a graph-like representation with nodes and edges (the lines linking nodes). This is why a semantic data model is often called an *RDF graph model*. A database that stores triples is called a *Triple Store*.

Semantic modeling simplifies handling sparse data and merging of data. We represent data as nodes (entities) and edges (relationships). This model can accommodate sparse data where not all entities have relationships with each other. This simplifies the handling of sparse data compared to rigid table structures like in relational databases.

Semantic modeling also simplifies the merging of data through relationship-based merging. When merging data from different sources or systems, the relationships between entities can be used as a natural way to integrate the data. Graph databases can merge data based on interconnectedness instead of relying solely on common keys or identifiers, as in relational databases. This simplifies the integration process as it leverages the inherent relationships between entities.

In summary, we should consider using semantic modeling when:

- The information is better represented through relationships

- Information belongs to more than one entity

- Deleting an entity should automatically delete all connected entities. If the data is modeled only as triples, the cascading effect of deletion can be fully automated through one SPARQL query. In case data is modeled as both triples and documents, the connected entities can be easily identified, and deletion can be performed.

- If data already available as triples

- We will display the entities and relationships on a user interface as a network graph. In this case, semantic modeling will be the best choice as a tabular view for relational data.

Since MarkLogic is a multi-model database, both triples and documents co-exist. For example, *"Shelly is a member of the Analytics Department"* can be modeled as shown in Figure 7.34.

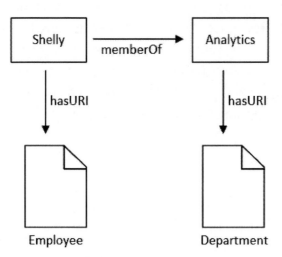

Figure 7.34: Triples and documents can co-exist.

Figure 7.34 shows an easily navigable *memberOf* relationship between entity instances *Shelly (User entity)* and *Analytics (Department Entity)*. The entity instance has an easily navigable relationship *hasURI* with the document with complete information about those entities. We can adopt the most suitable modeling approaches discussed above for modeling the Employee and Department entities.

When modeling relationships, we can use three types of abstraction processes:

- **Generalization** (is_a) – relationship of a subset between occurrences of two or more objects by using a 'is a' relations. An example would be "an employer is a generalization of managers."

- **Classification** (instance_of) – Classify entities based on similar characteristics. Like a group of employees. For example, "Shelly is an instance of Employee."

- **Aggregation** (has_a) - Defines a new object from a group of entities.

Implementing the Semantic Graph Pattern

As mentioned above, triples are the backbone of the Semantic Graph pattern. To implement the pattern, we need to model the triples. There are two variants of implementing the Semantic Graph Pattern using triples:

- Managed triples
- Unmanaged triples.

Managed triples

In the Managed triples variant, we load triples explicitly and MarkLogic figures out how to store them internally. With managed triples, MarkLogic functions like a triple store.

We can insert triple with the functions `sem:rdf-insert` (XQuery) or `sem.rdfInsert` (JavaScript).

```
xquery version "1.0-ml";
import module namespace sem =
"http://marklogic.com/semantics"
   at "/MarkLogic/semantics.xqy";
sem:rdf-insert(
(sem:triple(
sem:iri("http://example.org/article_1001"),
sem:iri("http://example.org/category"),
sem:iri("http://example.org/BI")
),
sem:triple(
sem:iri("http://example.org/article_1002"),
sem:iri("http://example.org/category"),
sem:iri("http://example.org/Databases")
)
))
declareUpdate();
const sem = require("/MarkLogic/semantics.xqy");
sem.rdfInsert([
 sem.triple(
  sem.iri("http://example.org/article_1001"),
  sem.iri("http://example.org/category"),
  sem.iri("http://example.org/BI")
  ),
 sem.triple(
  sem.iri("http://example.org/article_1002"),
  sem.iri("http://example.org/category"),
  sem.iri("http://example.org/Databases")
  )
])
```

After running the above code, XML documents are created in the database with URIs starting with `/triplestore/`, **and** a collection `http://marklogic.com/semantics#default-graph`.

The content of the document is like:
```
<sem:triples
xmlns:sem="http://marklogic.com/semantics">
    <sem:triple>
            <sem:subject>
            </sem:subject>
            <sem:predicate>
            </sem:predicate>
            <sem:object>
            </sem:object>
    </sem:triple>
    <sem:triple>
            <sem:subject>
            </sem:subject>
            <sem:predicate>
            </sem:predicate>
            <sem:object>
            </sem:object>
    </sem:triple>
</sem:triples>
```

There are two triples in this document, which we can show as:

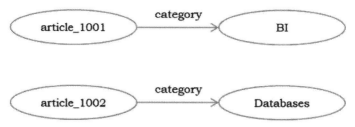

Figure 7.35: Managed Triples example.

In plain English, these triples represent two real-world scenarios:

"article_1001 has a category of BI"
"article_1002 has a category of Databases"

Refer to the MarkLogic documentation for more examples and options for the APIs.

If we need to insert triples from a location (file system or internet), then APIs `sem:rdf-load` (XQuery) or `sem.rdfLoad`(JavaScript) can be used.

Unmanaged triples

We can implement unmanaged triples in two ways:

Unmanaged triples as embedded triples

Triples that are included as part of an XML or a JSON document and have an element node of `sem:triple` or `sem.triple` are called *embedded triples*. These unmanaged triples must be in the MarkLogic XML or JSON format defined in the sem:triple or sem. triple schema.

With unmanaged triples, MarkLogic functions like both a triple store and a document store. Both triple and document store functionalities are available for the data inserted into MarkLogic.

Here, we insert an unmanaged triple into an XML document:

```
xquery version "1.0-ml";
import module namespace sem =
"http://marklogic.com/semantics"
at "/MarkLogic/semantics.xqy";
xdmp:document-insert("Article1001.xml",
   <article>
     <info>
     <title>Article Date Nov 1 2023</title>
     <sem:triples xmlns:sem="http://marklogic.
com/semantics">
```

```
        <sem:triple>
          <sem:subject>
            http://example.org/article_1001
          </sem:subject>
          <sem:predicate>
            http://example.org/category
          </sem:predicate>
          <sem:object datatype=
            "http://www.w3.org/2001/XMLSchema#string">
            BI
          </sem:object>
        </sem:triple>
    </sem:triples>
    </info>
  </article>
)
```

Here, we insert an unmanaged triple into a JSON document:

```
declareUpdate();
var sem = require("/MarkLogic/semantics. xqy");
var doc = {
"Article":{
  "title":"Article Date Nov 12 2023",
    "triple":{
      "subject":"http://example.org/article_1002",
      "predicate":"http://example.org/category",
      "object":{
    "datatype":http://www.w3.org/2001/XMLSchema#string
        "value": "Databases"
}}}}
xdmp.documentInsert("Article1002.json", doc)
```

The above code inserts `Article1001.xml` and `Article1002.json`. Each document also carries one triple, which corresponds to these real-world scenarios:

"article_1001 has a category of BI"
"article_1002 has a category of Databases"
We can also represent them in the same way.

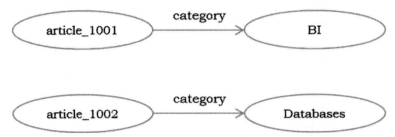

Figure 7.36: Unmanaged triples example.

The inserted documents will look like:

Article1001.xml

```
<article>
  <title>Article Date Nov 1 2023</title>
    <sem:triples xmlns:sem="http://marklogic.
com/semantics">
      <sem:triple>
        <sem:subject>
</sem:subject>
        <sem:predicate>
</sem:predicate>
        <sem:object
datatype="http://www.w3.org/2001/XMLSchema#string">
BI
        </sem:object>
      </sem:triple>
  </sem:triples>
</article>
```

Article1002.json

```
{
"Article": {
      "title": "Article Date Nov 12 2023",
  "triple": {
    "subject": "http://example.org/article_1002",
    "predicate": "http://example.org/category",
    "object": {
     "datatype":
     "http://www.w3.org/2001/XMLSchema#string",
     "value": "Databases"
    }
   }
  }
}
```

Compared to managed triples, the triples embedded in the XML and JSON documents have the same life span as the embedding document. When we delete the documents `Article1001.xml` or `Article1002.json`, we also delete the triples. Dropping managed triples should be explicitly done through SPARQL statements.

Other than the difference in managing the triples, interacting with the triples generated through both variants is the same way – through SPARQL queries. However, the difference in managing the triples between both variants is important from a modeling perspective.

Unmanaged triples extracted using a template

As mentioned, we typically generate unmanaged triples from information already available in the document. Identifying such triples can be automated using *Template Driven Extraction (TDE)*. Here, you define a template to identify data to be indexed as triples in an existing document. These triples behave as unmanaged or embedded triples because their life is as long as the document exists. We can apply simple data processing functions during the extraction process, like concatenating two or more XML properties or JSON elements to a single value, changing date formats, etc. The triples generated using TDEs cannot be physically seen in the document, but those triples can be queried using SPARQL.

Choosing between managed triples and unmanaged triples

Keep information close together if it belongs together. For instance, if the information in a document is enriched with additional information, it makes sense to embed those triples in the document. In other words, as unmanaged triples. An additional advantage is that it is easy to maintain the information. If the document is deleted, the triples get deleted automatically.

If the information comes from an entirely different source than the document data and stands on its own, storing the triples as managed triples makes more sense. Various standards bodies develop RDF vocabularies, ontologies, or taxonomies, which enterprises then utilize for tasks such as generating knowledge graphs or facilitating standardized information exchange, such as federal reporting. In such instances, we store external RDFs as managed triples within MarkLogic. Some examples of such RDF vocabularies are:

- SNOMED Clinical terms
- Fast HealthCare Interoperability Resources (FHIR)
- SportsML
- FOODIE Ontology
- Rail Topology Ontology

In a real-world scenario, RDF data often comprises a blend of generic information sourced from external sources and document-specific details enriched using internal data. In such instances, it's advisable to embed only the document-specific triples (unmanaged triples) while storing other triples separately (managed triples). The key point to highlight is the significant benefit derived from integrating these two realms. MarkLogic seamlessly accommodates plain documents (both XML and JSON), documents with embedded triples, and managed triples all within the same environment, facilitating efficient querying across them.

Applying the Semantic Graph Pattern to our case study

In the pet adoption use case, we can have a Pet document with embedded triples:

```
//Pet Document
{ "triples": [
  { "triple": {
      "subject": "http://pet.com/dog19370824",
      "predicate": "http://pet.com/isOfBreed",
      "object": "http://pet.com/breed101"
    }
  }],
  "petId": "dog19370824",
  "petName": "Fanny",
  "breeds": [
    { "code": "breed101",
      "name": "Dalmatian"
    }
  ]
}

//Breed Document
{ "triples": [
    {
      "triple": {
        "subject": "http://pet.com/breed101",
        "predicate": "http://pet.com/hasBreedURI",
        "object": "/breeds/breed101.json"
      }
    }
  ],
  "breedId": "breed101",
```

```
"breedName": "Dalmatian",
"breedOrigin": "Croatia",
"breeTraits": [
  "loyal to the family",
  "good with children"
]
}
```

When these two documents are inserted, two triples are generated, as shown in Figure 7.37.

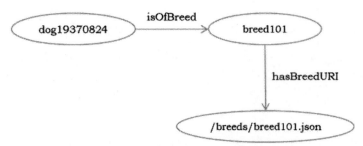

Figure 7.37: Unmanaged triples example.

Now, we have a natural connection from the dog entity to the breed entity. This SPARQL query navigates the relationship:

```
## query
PREFIX pet:<http://pet.com/>
SELECT ?breedURI
WHERE {
  pet:dog19370824 pet:isOfBreed ?breed.
  ?breed pet:hasBreedURI ?breedURI.
}
```

breedURI
</breeds/breed101.json>

Each document created one triple without explicitly attempting to connect between the Pet document and the Breed Document. We populate the embedded triples with the information available within that document itself. We establish the connection because the object of the embedded triple in the Pet document is the subject of the embedded triple in the Breed document. Such connections between entities can help develop knowledge graphs, visualize relationships in a network diagram, etc.

We can automatically generate the embedded triples created above using the *Template Driven Extraction (TDE)* method.

Benefits of the Semantic Graph Pattern

The main benefit of the Semantic Graph Pattern is that it helps create and maintain natural relationships between entities by modeling at a conceptual level rather than at the physical level. Other benefits include:

- **Interoperability**. The pattern promotes using standardized vocabularies and ontologies, and facilitates interoperability between different data sources and applications.

- **Semantic enrichment**. Semantic modeling patterns enable data enrichment with additional semantic metadata, enhancing its meaning and context. By annotating data with semantic tags and relationships, it becomes possible to infer new knowledge, make implicit relationships explicit, and thus support advanced querying and reasoning capabilities.

Trade-offs with the Semantic Graph Pattern

While the Semantic Graph Pattern offers a lot of benefits, there are trade-offs and challenges associated with its adoption:

- Understanding and working with RDF and OWL entail a learning curve for developers and users unfamiliar with semantic technologies.

- When the system generates billions of triples, close attention should be given to the resource, especially memory, because all triples are indexed in MarkLogic automatically.

- SPARQL is the natural query language that interacts with triples. In MarkLogic, the best practice is using document and semantic models together. Mixing document and SPARQL queries might require special skills, especially in writing performant SPARQL queries.

- Data in triples could duplicate information that is already in the document.

Summary of the Semantic Graph Pattern

The Semantic Modeling Pattern offers a powerful approach to data modeling and representation, promoting interoperability, reusability, flexibility, and semantic enrichment. Organizations should also consider some trade-offs and challenges with respect to learning curves and skill sets while adopting the Semantic Modeling Pattern.

Problem	• Relationships between entities are hard to represent
	• Implicit relationships which needs complex reasoning to identify
Solution	• Generate triples that represents relationships between entities
Use cases	• Knowledge Graphs
	• Fraud Detection
	• Recommendation Systems
	• Publishing
Benefits	• Easy way to represent relationships
	• Interoperability
	• Semantic Enrichment
Trade-offs	• Potentially creates data duplication
	• Need of specialized skills
	• Potentially could be resource heavy

Table 7.19: The Semantic Graph Pattern.

Primary keys

In a relational database, the primary key serves as a unique identifier for a record. MarkLogic adopts the primary key concept, albeit with a notable difference from traditional relational databases. In MarkLogic, a document corresponds to a row in a relational database and its unique identifier is the document URI. Technically, no XML element, attribute, or JSON property inside the document serves as a unique identifier.

Ultimately, composing the URI is a data modeling exercise. The following are some best practices on how to construct a URI:

- Make the URI meaningful not only to provide context but understanding for those who follow.

- Words used in the URI should be nouns or collective nouns.

- If the data changes state over time, indicating state/status in the URI can be beneficial.

- The URI reads left-to-right with increased specificity.

- Organize the nodes in the URI like a folder structure with parts quickly identifiable.

- If a primary key exists in the document, it's advisable to incorporate it into the URI.

- Sensitive data, like PII data, should not be used in the URI.

- Source name and ingest time for raw capture may contribute to the URI path.

- Spaces must be converted to hyphens.

Examples:

1. Using the pet context, the primary key is "petId" which leads to a suitable URI such as.

Figure 7.38: A better URI.

Note that we can document the URI pattern in Hackolade Studio.

2. Documents representing employees in the HR department of organization ABC could have URIs like "/abc/hr/employees/10001.json."

This example follows the general pattern: "/prefix(es)/<uniqueId>.<suffix>," where prefixes can be structured to organize documents, akin to a folder structure.

Additional items to note:

- It is prudent to consider future needs when devising the URI strategy to ensure suitability. While altering the URIs of existing documents is feasible, it entails significant effort.

- The default behavior of MarkLogic is to silently overwrite the document if a document with the same URI comes in. This behavior is overridden only in the case of temporal documents where the application works on a base URI and MarkLogic creates versions of the existing documents with a different URI.

- Except for the bulk ingestion tool, MarkLogic Content Pump (MLP), there is no mechanism to autogenerate unique URIs in MarkLogic. The ingesting application should determine the URI or should be a programmatically generated one. There are APIs like sem:uuid/sem.uuid, sem:uuid-string()/sem.uuidString to assist with generating URIs.

- If known, using a suffix representing the type of document (.xml, json, .txt) is highly recommended. Otherwise, MarkLogic inspects the content and understands the type for indexing purposes. If it cannot understand, the document will be assumed to be of binary type and will not be indexed.

Monitoring schema evolution

Organizations operate in different ways. In many organizations following the principles in this book, data modeling happens in the initial stages of an Agile sprint or due to an application change, and then code changes occur and are implemented in different environments.

In other organizations, development has the upper hand, and evolutions tend to happen in a code-first manner. In such cases, data modeling can still come in handy to help with data quality and consistency. We discuss *retroactive data modeling* or *data modeling after-the-fact*.

This process is useful for identifying inconsistencies, such as the presence of addresses using the field *zipcode* while others use *postalcode*. It is also critical to identify potentially more damaging situations in the area of PII, GDPR, confidentiality, etc.

Hackolade Studio provides a command-line interface to programmatically invoke many of the features available in the graphical user interface. It is easy to orchestrate a succession of commands. In a code-first approach, the structure in the database instance evolves first. Every night, a scheduled process goes through the following steps:

- Reverse-engineer the database instance.

- Compare the resulting model with the baseline model. This produces a "delta model" and, optionally, a *merged model*.

- A manual step allows us to review the model comparison and identify whether all changes in production are legitimate. Adjustments might be necessary to the code, or data needs migration.

- Commit the merged model, which becomes the new baseline model, resulting in publication to the corporate data dictionary to make business users aware of the evolution.

Schema migration

We have mentioned many times the great flexibility of the MarkLogic document when it comes to easily modifying the schema as application requirements evolve. Compared to relational databases, achieving this with zero downtime, without the infamous migration weekends, or without blue/green deployments and other complex approaches is simple.

We have also highlighted the need to leverage the Schema Versioning Pattern to help applications process the data with the appropriate business rules and enable backward compatibility.

Challenges quickly arise in large and complex environments, particularly when multiple applications read the same data. It is not efficient or practical to port convoluted business logic to multiple applications for dozens of schema evolutions over time. It even ends up burning useless CPU cycles to handle them. There are also risks of misinterpretation and misguided business decisions due to a query that is unaware of some specific schema evolution.

New users of MarkLogic discovering the flexibility of the document model often don't realize that it is a best practice in successful organizations to scrupulously perform schema migrations to reduce the technical debt of maintaining old schema versions in the data.

There are several schema migration strategies to consider. The choice of strategy will depend on the specific needs of the database and the business, and careful planning and testing are essential to ensure a successful migration. Some organizations are even known to have developed costing models to evaluate the tradeoffs of the different strategies.

We can classify schema migration strategies into two basic approaches: eager migration and lazy migration (there are also hybrid strategies that combine aspects of both):

- **Eager migration**. Schema changes are made all at once, and the data is migrated to the new schema immediately. Similar to what we do with relational databases, this approach requires more planning and may result in downtime during the migration process. Still, it ensures that all data is immediately updated to the new schema.

- **Lazy migration**. Schema changes are made incrementally, and the data is migrated to the new schema only when it is accessed or updated. This approach can be less disruptive and easier to implement but adds latency to common operations. Furthermore, it is possible that we may never migrate all the data to the new schema.

- **Predictive migration**. Schema changes are made based on predictions of how to use data in the future. This approach requires more planning and analysis but can minimize the latency in common operations.

- **Incremental migration**. Schema changes are made in small, iterative steps, and the data is progressively migrated to the new schema.

We can offload both predictive and incremental migration to processes running in the background and/or during off-peak hours to minimize system impact. You may also combine strategies depending on the remaining data to migrate; start with a predictive migration while doing lazy migration opportunistically, then finish with incremental migration.

Step 3: Optimize

Similar to indexing, denormalizing, partitioning, and adding views to a RDBMS physical model, we would add database-specific features to the query refinement model to produce the query design model.

Indexing

Nowadays, businesses handle vast volumes of data every day. Databases offer a secure, dependable, and enduring storage layer for this data. Simultaneously, there is a need for rapid data delivery to users making requests. Within databases, indexes serve as data structures that enhance data access efficiency. Indexes are optional; the databases can operate properly without indexes. However, not efficiently. Indexes play a crucial role in accelerating query processing by swiftly providing access to the data we need to include in the response. Whether databases are relational or non-relational, they generally perceive indexes similarly, and MarkLogic is no exception. However, because MarkLogic is a search-ready database, it incorporates automated and advanced indexing techniques to enhance the search query processing.

MarkLogic supports a variety of index types.

The Universal Index

This is the default index in MarkLogic and cannot be dropped. The universal index indexes the XML elements and JSON properties of loaded documents. The universal index indexes text, structure, and combinations of text and structure found in collections of JSON and XML documents. It is optimized to combine text, structure, and value searches into a single process for high-performance search queries. The most important feature is that MarkLogic doesn't require advanced knowledge of the document structure nor completely adhere to a particular schema. This makes the ingestion process very easy, and the ingested documents are immediately available for Google-like search as well as structure-aware search using XPath expressions. Below is the comprehensive list of *things* included in the Universal Index:

- Words
- Phrases
- Document structure
- Values
- Document metadata
  - Collections
  - Directory
  - Properties
  - Permissions
  - Metadata values

Range indexes

MarkLogic maintains a universal index for each database, enabling rapid searches for text, structure, and their combinations within collections of XML and JSON documents. Nevertheless, when XML and JSON documents contain numeric or date information, queries involving conditions like inequalities (e.g., price >=

100.00 AND date >= <a date>) may arise. Specifying range indexes of these elements, attributes, or JSON properties substantially increases the evaluation of such queries. Table 7.20 shows different types of range indexes.

Type	Description
Element Range Index	A range index on an XML element or JSON property
Attribute range index	A range index on an attribute in an XML element
Path range index	A range index on an XML element, XML attribute, or JSON property as defined by an XPath expression
Field range index	A range index on a field

Table 7.20: Different types of range indexes.

Creating range indexes should be done explicitly through Admin Interface, the XQuery or JavaScript Admin API, or the REST Management API. Range indexes are populated during the document loading process and are automatically updated with subsequent updates to the indexed data. It is important to define range indexes for a database before loading XML or JSON documents that contain the content to be indexed. Otherwise, the content must be re-indexed or reloaded to take advantage of the new range indexes.

Path range indexes

Path range indexes are useful in circumstances in which an element or attribute range index will not work. For example, you may have documents with the same element name appearing under different parent elements and you want only to index the elements appearing under one of the parent elements. In this case, a path range index is required to correctly index that element. For example, suppose we have two documents:

```
{
  "User": {
  "id": 1001,
  "firstName": "Tom",
  "lastName": "Swiss",
  "type": "Customer"
  }
}

{
  "User": {
  "id": 9001,
  "firstName": "Blaire",
  "lastName": "Scarth",
  "type": "Employee"
  }
}
```

If an element range index for `"id"` is created, then both 1001 and 9001 will be indexed. But, if the requirement needs to only index ids of employees, then a Path Range Index for below path is required:

```
/User[type = "Employee"]/id
```

Geospatial indexes

MarkLogic supports two categories of geospatial queries (Point query, Region query). For best performance, the geospatial queries should be backed by a geospatial index or a geospatial region index. Geospatial indexes are required for faster performance of point queries. A geospatial region index is required for the performance of region queries. Based on where the geospatial data is

located in a XML or JSON document, different categories
of geospatial indexes are available. They all behave the
same way but differ based on where the geospatial data
is modeled in the XML or JSON document.

Type	Description

Geospatial Element Index	Used when the latitude and longitude values are in a single XML element or JSON property separated by whitespace or punctuation.
	`<coords>49.42,-122.43</coords>`
	`"coords":"49.42, -122.43"`

Geospatial Element Child Index	Used when the coordinates are contained in an XML element or JSON property and the container element or property is a child of another element of property.
	
	`<location>`
	`  <coords>49.42,-122.43</coords>`
	`</location>`
	
	`"location": {`
	`  "coords":"49.42, -122.43"`
	`}`

Geospatial Element Pair Index	Used when the latitude and longitude are in separate elements or properties.
	
	`<location>`
	`  <lat>49.42</lat>`
	`  <long>-122.43</long>`
	`</location>`
	
	`"location": {`
	`  "lat":49.42,`
	`  "long": -122.43`
	`}`

Geospatial Attribute Pair Index	Used when the latitude and longitude values are in two different attributes of the same XML parent element. `<location lat="49.42" long="-122.43" />`

Type	Description

Geospatial Path Index	Used when there is a need to express the location of the points using XPath expression. For example, if the document is:
	
	 `<a:data>`
	`  <a:geo>37.52 -122.25</a:geo>`
	`</a:data>`
	 the indexing path expression is
	 `/a:data/a:geo`

Table 7.21: Types of geospatial indexes.

Geospatial region path indexes are used to index geospatial regions, such as polygons, rather than points. Table 7.22 shows examples of the index path expressions in different scenarios.

Document	Indexing Path Expression

`<a:location>`
`<a:region>`
`  POLYGON ((30 10,`
`           40 40,`
`           20 40,`
`           10 20,`
`           30 10))`
`</a:region>`
`</a:location>`
	`/a:location/a:region`

`<a:location>`
`<a:loc region="POLYGON ((`
`          30 10,`
`          40 40,`
`          20 40,`
`          10 20,`
`          30 10))"`
`/>`
`</a:location>`
	`/a:location/a:loc/@region`

Document	Indexing Path Expression

`{"location": {`
`    "region": "POLYGON ((`
`                30 10,`
`                40 40,`
`                20 40,`
`                10 20,`
`                30 10`
`            ))"`
`}}`
	`/location/region`

Table 7.22: Geospatial region path index.

Triple indexes

Universal and range indexes are essential to enhance document searches. Similarly, triple indexes play a crucial role in optimizing semantic searches. MarkLogic requires support for search patterns representing triples to facilitate semantic search, thus necessitating a slightly distinct index structure.

There are three special indexes for semantic search:

1. Triple index
2. Triple values index
3. Triple type index.

The triple index preserves triple representations. Triple indexing occurs upon ingesting or updating documents containing sem:triple XML elements or triple JSON properties. Unique values are stored once in a dictionary within the triple index. Each value is assigned an ID in the dictionary, utilized by triple data to reference the corresponding value.

Conceptually, each index entry comprises three columns representing a triple's subject, object, and predicate, alongside a column mapping the triple to its respective document. Additionally, columns for positional information (if we enable the *triple positions* configuration property in the database) are included. The order of storing triple elements significantly affects MarkLogic's efficiency in resolving semantic searches. Consequently, we store each triple in three permutations within the triple index: subject-object-predicate (SOP), predicate-subject-object (PSO), and object-predicate-subject (OPS). A designated column specifies the permutation, enabling optimized search performance.

The triple index doesn't directly store values (IRIs or literals) from each triple. Instead, it uses integer IDs for expedited lookups. We map actual values to these IDs in the *triple value index*. MarkLogic reconstructs their values by referencing the triple value index while retrieving triples from the triple index for search results. Consequently, MarkLogic only needs to access the triple indexes to yield semantic query results, enhancing retrieval speed.

Triples often include typed literal values (strings, dates, numbers, etc.). MarkLogic utilizes the type information and stores it in a *triple type index*. A null value in the triple type index indicates an IRI.

We can summarize the above details with an example. Suppose we have this triple:

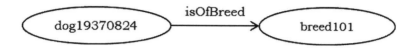

Figure 7.39: Example RDF triple.

Figure 7.40 shows how we can conceptually represent the triple indexes for this triple (assuming triple positions are turned on).

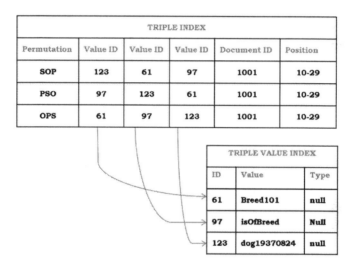

Figure 7.40: Conceptual representation of triple indexes.

MarkLogic handles all triple indexing complexities internally. The SPARQL engine matches the patterns in a SPARQL query, finding the triples from indexes and joining them for the final result. For example, a SPARQL query filtering on dog19370824 would first search the triple value index and then find the related predicates and objects by id using the triple index. In the above example, a triple type index is not created as the type is a string literal.

Having a basic grasp of the index structure is valuable for crafting efficient SPARQL queries and determining hardware requirements as the volume of triples grows. It's important to note that each triple corresponds to three entries in the triple index dictionaries – SOP, PSO, and OPS. Future MarkLogic revisions might support more permutations like SPO.

There are many reasons to use a data modeling tool to create and maintain indexing information, including better collaboration, documentation, ease of maintenance, and better governance. In addition to supporting all of the indexing options of MarkLogic, Hackolade Studio also generates the index syntax to apply to the database instance or gives it to an administrator to apply.

Generation of test data

Manually generating fake data for testing and demos takes time and slows the testing process, particularly if large volumes are required.

Using fake (a.k.a synthetic) data can be useful during system development, testing, and demos, mainly because it avoids using real identities, full names, real credit card numbers or Social Security Numbers, etc., while using "Lorem ipsum" strings and random numbers is not realistic enough to be meaningful.

Alternatively, one could use cloned production data, except it generally does not exist for new applications.

Plus, you would still have to mask or substitute sensitive data to avoid disclosing any personally identifiable information. Synthetic data is also useful for exploring edge cases lacking real data or identifying model bias.

With Hackolade Studio, you can generate first names and last names that look real but are not, and the same for company names, product names and descriptions, street addresses, phone numbers, credit card numbers, commit messages, IP addresses, UUIDs, image names, URLs, etc.

The data generated here may be fake, but has the expected format and contains meaningful values. City and street names, for example, are randomly composed from elements that mimic real names. You can set the desired locale so the data elements are localized for better contextual meaning.

Generating mock test data is a 2-step process:

- One-time setup for each model: you must associate each attribute with a function to get a contextually realistic sample

- Each time you need to generate test data, you define the parameters of the run

Hackolade Studio generates sample documents so they can be inserted into the database instance.

Four tips

1. **Access pattern analysis:** Define how you plan to access/query the documents at the beginning of the data modeling process, not towards the end.

2. **Workload analysis:** Estimates of the volume and velocity of access patterns have a major impact on your choice of schema design patterns. It may evolve over time, sometimes requiring the schema's and corresponding application code's refactoring. Fortunately, the JSON-like document model makes it much easier to evolve schema with MarkLogic than for relational databases.

3. **Schema versioning:** It is not a matter of if your schema will evolve, but when. Changing customer needs, new strategic direction, unforeseen requirements, scope creep, continuous enhancements, iterative development, etc. It is a fact of life that your schema design will evolve over time. So you might as well organize yourself for that.

4. **Schema migration:** After baking cookies, one generally cleans the dishes and puts away the utensils. Don't forget to migrate your documents to the new schema version to eliminate the technical debt of schema evolution.

Three takeaways

1. **Data modeling is even more important for MarkLogic than for relational databases:** The flexibility of JSON and XML, along with the ease of evolution, provide a false sense of security, as there are no guardrails like the normalization rules in relational databases. The consequence is that the responsibility to ensure consistency, integrity, and quality shifts elsewhere. The section earlier in this book illustrates the number of different ways one can design a schema. You must choose the appropriate pattern(s) wisely based on information gathered in the Align and Refine phases.

2. **Gather knowledge and experience from different stakeholders and domain experts:** Developers might be tempted to design schemas themselves. There's no doubt that they possess the technical knowledge to design a schema for a JSON or XML document. However, to avoid reworking the application code, it is more efficient to first understand the different constraints based on the analysis of the access patterns, the workload, the application flow, and the screen wireframes. Using a diagramming tool like Hackolade Studio facilitates the conversation with non-technical stakeholders and helps reduce the time-to-market of application development efforts.

3. **Data tends to outlive applications by a wide margin:** It might be tempting to think that application code is where we document schemas

and enforce quality. But multiple applications probably share data, plus the lifespan of applications is much shorter than for data. Hence, it is critical to ensure a shared understanding of the meaning and context of data beyond a single application. Data modeling and schema design for MarkLogic help achieve this objective.

Index

---

[i] JSON Schema - https://json-schema.org/

[ii] XML Schema - https://www.w3.org/TR/xmlschema11-1/

Made in the USA
Columbia, SC
16 September 2024

41861134R00187